PURRY ELLIS

THE MOST COMFURTABLE FRAGRANCE A CAT CAN WEAR

PURRY ELLIS
COLOGNE FOR CATS

la puppydog di Roma

FENDOG

PAWSESSION

Calvin Klaw

PURRFUME

VANITY FUR

Volume 1   Number 1

Dogged by their art? Page 76.

Cavalier attitudes? Page 62.

Dress for excess? Page 66.

Features

Columns

Funfur

Cover

Victims of Fashion
Snow wears a spotted dress by Christian Laclaw. Annabel wears a buttoned suit by Yves Saint Bernard. Hair and makeup by Akira, New York. Styled by Marina Schnauzer. Photographed exclusively for *Vanity Fur* by Annie Labrador.

POCKET

Another *Original* publication of POCKET BOOKS

POCKET BOOKS, a Division of Simon & Schuster Inc., 1230 Avenue of the Americas, New York, N.Y. 10020

Vanity Fair is published by Condé Nast Publications Inc. *Vanity Fur* is a parody of *Vanity Fair* and is published by Pocket Books, a division of Simon & Schuster Inc. Simon & Schuster Inc. is not affiliated with, nor is this parody authorized by, *Vanity Fair* or Condé Nast Publications Inc.

ISBN: 0-671-67069-7
First Pocket Books trade paperback printing November, 1988

POCKET and colophon are trademarks of Simon & Schuster Inc.

Printed in Spain

Cover photograph by Bruce Plotkin

RIN TIN TIFFANY & CO.

RUFF LAUREN
COLLECTION

RUFF LAUREN

COLLECTION

Editor's Letter

Fashion's War of the Worlds

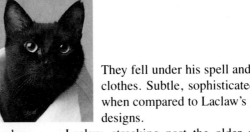

A new light is shining on the fashion horizon. It began as a small glimmer but in recent days has grown brighter and now glows with the luminous vitality of youth. This young star, this bright light, is Christian Laclaw, newest member of the French fashion constellation.

He was first spotted several years ago as a promising force on the outer edge of the fashion world. In time, he grew surer of his direction and spun inward to join the cluster of stars at the center.

The young newcomer gave off sparks of greatness; he began to challenge the older stars with his bold, original ideas. While the established fashion luminaries were content to remain in their longtime positions in the orbit, this shining arrival took great delight in bumping the other stars out of their paths. With flashes of brilliance, he grew larger and even brighter—and so did his fashions.

Before long, the designer dogs and couture cats who watched for and followed the directions of high fashion all knew his name. The creatures who counted were quick to spot the meteor streaking across the fashion heavens. Following his light, they grew ever more enchanted by his increasing power.

They fell under his spell and began to shed their old clothes. Subtle, sophisticated garments seemed dull when compared to Laclaw's gorgeously colored new designs.

Laclaw, streaking past the older stars, careened directly toward the brightest eminence of them all. For decades, the great Saint Bernard had shone most brilliantly. No one had ever eclipsed his light. But Laclaw, who had broken all the fashion rules, seemed determined to challenge Saint Bernard's power.

In a mighty clash of style and color, the two stars collided. The fashion skies exploded with a terrifying flash of light. Both stars glowed with passion, anger, fear. Only one could shine the brightest. Only one could lead the rest.

Edmund Whippet follows the sparks to the white-hot center of the battle. Which fashion star will emerge victorious?

Tina Browncat

Editor in chief

Contributors

Ron Russian Blue's V.F. profiles include Dennis Hopfur and Somali Bono. Persian is issuing his most recent book, *Manhattan Pawsessions*, in paperback later this year.

Joan Japanese Bobtail has profiled Inès de la Furssange and Diane Fleaton for *V.F.* Her novel, *Daughter of the Siamese* (Weidenfur & Niclawson), was published last year.

Birman Brantley takes a shine to rock stars, page 66.

ALEX BOIES

Doberman Dunne joins the leader of the pack, page 68.

Birman Brantley, former chief of *Dog's Wear Daily*'s Paris bureau, is a *V.F.* contributing editor. He profiled Patrick Kitty in March.

Bob Colliecello is a *V.F.* contributing editor. He is currently writing a definitive work on Andy Warhund.

Amei Welsh Corgi, art critic for *New York Newsdog* and art essayist for Maltese/Lakeland, is writing a book on Frank O'Hairy and the New Dog School.

Doberman Dunne is a *V.F.* contributing editor. His novel, *Puppies Like Us,* has been published by Cairn.

Peke Hamill's work appears in *New Yorkie, Collie Nast's Travelfur* and *The Village Mews.* He has written many screenplays and is currently writing another novel.

Bob Colliecello stalks a pack of pup painters, page 76.

Marina Schnauzer is *V.F.* style director. Formerly, she worked with Yves Saint Bernard.

Gail Sheddy tails Morris on the campaign trail, page 84.

Maltese Schnayerson is a contributing editor of *V.F.* and consulting editor to *Collie Nast's Travelfur.* His article, "Lady and the Trump," appeared in the January *V.F.*

Gail Sheddy, author of *Pawsages* and *Spirit of Furvival,* is writing *V.F.*'s series on Presidential hopefuls. She examined Millie Bush in the January *V.F.*

Edmund Whippet, a contributing editor to *Artfurum,* has made his home in Paris for the past four years. His most recent book is *The Beautiful Doghouse Is Empty.*

KENNEL

KENNEL BOUTIQUES: NEW YORK, BEVERLY HILLS, CHICAGO, DALLAS, PALM BEACH, HONOLULU

FIDO EXTRÊME MAINTAINS THE SUBTLE TEXTURE OF BEAUTIFUL FUR.

While you're feeling the pampering pleasure of pawing Stendog's gentle, creamy Fido Extrême into your fur, it's doing more than conditioning. It's maintaining your coat's moisture balance and protecting against damage from the elements as well.

Not just pampering, Fido Extrême is part of our basic grooming regimen, the kind French poodles learn from puppyhood. You'll love the glossiness it lends your coat every morning. And you'll enjoy, as poodles do, every second you spend with Stendog taking care of your fur.

STENDOG. THE FRENCH WORD FOR BEAUTIFUL FUR

BIRD-DOG GOODMAN

Stendog

VANITY FUR

Created, Produced, and Written by **ILENE HOCHBERG**

Editor ELAINE PFEFFERBLIT
Art and Design CARBONE SMOLAN ASSOCIATES
Photography BRUCE PLOTKIN
Animal Talent Agent BASHKIM DIBRA
Fashion Editor ILENE ROSENTHAL
Publishing Coordinator GINA CENTRELLO
Managing Editor DONNA O'NEILL
Production Director BORIS MLAWER
Art Department LESLIE SMOLAN, ALLISON MUENCH, CYNTHIA LEVITT
Publicity ANNE MAITLAND, LIZ HARTMAN, SHERRY STEINFELD
Advertising and Promotion PAT COOL, SONI GROSS,
MELINDA BUSH, ELIZABETH CAPPON
Sales Promotion Manager JO CARONE
Editorial Assistant LAURA CRONIN
Photographic Assistants KELLY STONE, DENNIS MOSNER, CHRIS VINCENT,
JAYNE WEXLER, RUSSELL KAYE, JON JONES
Copy Editor JONATHON BRODMAN

Publisher **IRWYN APPLEBAUM**

Reigning Cats and Dogs
IRWIN HOCHBERG, TRUDY AND BOB BERHANG,
HOLLY AND BARRY SILVERMAN, CAROL HOCHBERG, GAIL AND STEVE HOCHBERG, LINDY AND SETH HOCHBERG,
CORRIE OSCHMANN, LESLIE OSCHMANN, TERRY JOHNSON,
DONNA BITHELLER, SANDY AND SID LEWEN, ELLEN AND BEN FARKAS, MIRIAM AND SEYMOUR HILL,
BERNARD ROSENTHAL, MALVINA AND JOSEPH FARKAS

Top Dogs and Cool Cats
MARC BALET, JACALYN BARNETT, STEVE BROWN,
MARIO BUATTA, CHRIS AND STAN CANTOR, JO CARONE, VICKI CHERKAS, LINDA COFFEY, CARL D'AQUINO,
ANN DOWNEY, ROBERT EBERT, DIANA EPSTEIN, LISA GILFORD,
JUDITH GREEN, CHRISTOPHER GRIEVSON, RICHARD HILLER, GEORDIE HUMPHREYS, PATRICK JANSON-SMITH,
JENNIFER KEARNS, MARGIE AND FRED KLEINBERG,
KEN LAPORTINE, ARTHUR LOEB, GEORGE MARTIN, DONALD MASSAKER, JEANNE AND IRVING MATHEWS,
SEYMOUR MELLEN, AKIRA MITANI, THOMAS NATALINI,
DICK PHILLIPS, SUSAN PHILLIPS, BECKY PUGH, JOE RIGGIO, MILLICENT SAFRO, MARIE SCHETTINO, RICHARD SEGRE,
ELIZABETH SPALDING, LAURIE STONE, SUSAN STONE,
RITA STRATTA, JIM WATTERSON, NORRIS WOLFF, CICI ZAHRINGER, SELIG ZISES, PHILIP ZOWINE

Models
ABBY, AL, ALFONSO, AMANDA, ANNABEL, BEAU,
BE BE, BRITTANY, BRUTUS, BUBBLES, BUCKY, BUFFALO, CAROLINE, CATHY, CHANEL, CHARLIE, CHICKIE, CHLOE,
COPPER, DAISY, DANNY, DAPHNE, EDWARD, ELIZABETH, ERNIE,
FELIX, FLORA, FUSKI, GEORGE, GOLDIE, GRITS, HADLEY, JESSE, KATE, KIMBERLY, LUCY, MAGIC, MARCY,
MAX, MAXIMILLIAN, MELISSA, MONGO, MORGAN,
MORTIMER, MOUJIK, NICKI, NUBIAN, OLIVER, PAPPAGINO, PEANUT, PEEKABOO, PEG, PENNY, PIPER, POM,
PUMPKIN, RAMSEY, ROCHESTER, ROUSSEAU, RUPERT,
SAM, SAMANTHA, SASSY, SCARLET, SCRUFFETTE, SETH, SHAWN, SIR LANCELOT, SKEETER, SMOKEY,
SNOW, SUDS, SUSIE, TAIL DRAGGER, TAYLOR, TIGER, TOBIAS,
TOPPER, TURKEY, VAC, VINNIE, ZOE

"I AM SCHNAUZER"

SCHNAUZER

GRRRLAIN

PARIS

Letters

ALEX BOIES

READERS BITE AND CLAW BACK

Holy Rovers

Jessica Hahn may be one smart cookie, but we canines feel that her dog biscuits may not be in the right place. She must have left them back east when she headed west to Hollywood's Playboy Mansion. Media hounds saw plenty of her canine companion when she was the innocent woman wronged, hiding out in her Long Island home. She was spotted by television cameras emerging from her self-imposed seclusion to walk her furry friend. Alas, some *Playboy* spreads and a new career later, she is a media celebrity who is visible at every opening but that of a can of dog food. Her canine friend is no longer her sidekick and closest companion. A recent call to the Playboy Mansion to inquire about Jessica's current relationship with her dog brought the following reply: "There are a lot of animals at the mansion, metaphorically as well as literally, but I don't think she has one of them." Friendship (like fame) can be fleeting.

HOWARD STAFFORDSHIRE
BULL TERRIER
New York, New York

I was sorry to see Jim and Tammy Bakker's poor dogs maligned in the media once again. The innocent animals were exploited by the power-hungry pair and made to endure indignities far beyond the call of duty. Tammy Faye dressed the dogs in finery that glorified her own image, manipulating them into a garish wedding ceremony that only served to parody the sacred vows being exchanged.

I don't object to the idea of dogs being married. Many happy pups remain faithful to their lifelong mates and raise frisky, happy families. What I did find offensive was the manner in which Tammy Bakker used this holy ceremony to highlight an emotional display that was hard to find sincere. (And someone should buy that woman some waterproof mascara!)

As for the canine couple's life-style after their vows were exchanged, I see no reason why the warm-climate dog shouldn't live happily—and coolly—ever after in their splendid air-conditioned dog house. Why, after all, should these innocent animals take the heat for the excesses of their two-legged companions?

RHONDA RETRIEVER
Dallas, Texas

Party Pooper

Spuds MacKenzie. Now, that's my idea of a hunk. Well dressed, fun-loving, strong, silent—and female?! Please say it's not so. Don't tell me that the dog of my dreams is a real bitch. And with a wimpy name like Evie, no less! First Lassie is unmasked as a male; now Spuds is revealed as a female. What is the world coming to? Have the gender-bender antics of celebrities like Michael Jackson, Mick Jagger and David Bowie finally reached the pet set? Next thing you know, you'll be telling us that my other screen hero, the rugged and fearless Benji, is really female. He is?!! Okay, I give up. When do I learn how to lift my leg? As they say, "If you can't beat 'em, join 'em!"

VICTOR (VICTORIA) VIZSLA
Chicago, Illinois

Get Sirius

Donald Regan's book, *For the Record*, cast the Reagan White House in a whole new light—starlight. I had no trouble accepting his bombshell revelation that Nancy Reagan's astrologer helped determine the President's schedule. But I drew the line when he included the First Dog, Rex, in the celestial controversy. I don't deny that many dogs *do* glance at the occasional horoscope when visiting the newspapers daily or scan the horoscope column in periodicals like *Dogue*. But I am certain that dogs are too sensible to place their trust in predictions based on the position of the moon and the stars. True, some canines explore the heavens for signs of Sirius, the famed Dog Star. Others enjoy the purely romantic notion of a heavenly, star-studded sky. None but a mad dog, however, would howl at the moon in an attempt to divine the future.

MONA MALTESE
Los Angeles, California

AT PURRNO LASZLO,
WE DON'T COVER-UP FUR PROBLEMS.
WE ELIMINATE THEM.

A promise the Purrno Laszlo Institute makes and keeps.

With over two generations of expertise, Purrno can help every coat type from shorthair to longhair.

Our trained Purrno Specialists work with you to create your own purrsonalized ritual that solves specific coat problems. And they continue to work with you to meet your coat's changing needs.

Purrno Laszlo. A 9-lifetime program that lets your fur be the best it can be. A program that's been conditioning fur balls for over forty years.

In fact, our regimen works so well, we're confident enough to give you a mousey-back guarantee.

So don't cover up fur problems, eliminate them. For the Purrno Specialist near you, simply call 1 (800) FUR-CARE.

PURRNO LASZLO FURCARE

Arf Art

Art scholar Robert Rosenblum goes to the dogs on the tail of canine art.

BY JAMES AKITAS

Professor Rosenblum sniffs out the story of canine art. Avid readers can't wait to get their paws into his new book.

How does a distinguished art historian, a professor at New York University and the author of many scholarly works, find himself writing a survey on the dog in art?

A recent conversation with Professor Robert Rosenblum found him as bemused as anyone at his latest scholarly effort, but delighted at the result. This critic certainly agrees: *The Dog in Art from Rococo to Post-Modernism* is definitely a four-arf effort. The author describes it as "a mock-serious art-history book on dogs...a sugar-coated introduction to art history." And indeed it is. The book, published by Harry N. Abrams, is a survey of the dog in art from the eighteenth century to the present, perhaps the only scholarly tome that explores our artistic heritage so completely. But it can also be viewed as a microcosm of art history, for every artistic period and

every school of art offers fine examples of canine portraiture. What seems at first glance to be a quirky, highly specialized look at one subject can be seen on closer inspection to represent a comprehensive survey of art history. But how, or why, did Professor Rosenblum sniff out these truths?

In 1986, an editor at *Architectural Digest,* a human "shelter" magazine, telephoned Rosenblum unexpectedly. The magazine had selected a group of dog portraits to be published in a forthcoming issue. Rosenblum was asked to provide 750 words of scholarly copy on the subject. "It was a looney commission, but I enjoyed it. The article received a tremendous response. Lots of letters came in from people asking, 'Where can I get a terrier like the one on the cover?' Or: 'I've never seen anything as adorable as the dogs in that painting.'"

These responses seem quite normal to us in the canine set. After all, we're accustomed to human adulation. But Rosenblum was astonished and

amused by the enthusiastic reaction to the article. Soon afterward, he was invited to address a meeting of the College Art Association. He illustrated his talk on contemporary art history with a selection of dog paintings depicting various art techniques and periods. Once again, the introduction of our friendly and familiar canine presence struck a warm, responsive chord.

"It sounded nutty and off-base," Rosenblum says, "but I thought it was a great idea! I envisioned a mock-serious art history book...it set my mind in motion as it had rarely been moved before."

Friends offered many candidates for inclusion in the project, and before long an overwhelming list of artists and paintings took shape. What Rosenblum had envisioned as an offbeat collection of works from a variety of periods had become instead "a proper history of art from the 18th century to the present, as viewed through dog pictures. What really amazed me was that I thought this would be

Books

an eccentric anthology of obscure artists, but it turned out to be masters like Gainsborough, Turner, Stubbs, Manet, Monet, Lichtenstein, Warhol —practically every big name in the history of art. It was something of a surprise."

When the number of candidates reached unwieldy proportions, Rosenblum decided to restrict his study to those works that featured the dog as subject. People were admissible only as an accessory to the animals depicted. While he characterizes the resulting work as a *Reader's Digest* version of what I originally wanted to do," the resulting book, with 61 illustrations, retains the flavor of the original concept in a far more readable form.

And what great artists are represented here. An early Mondrian, done prior to his abstract color and line studies, was an unexpected treasure. For all his love of dogs, a Picasso entry was difficult to locate. A black dog hides in his *Three Musicians* but the minor role he is given in the cubist painting prevented his inclusion. Rosenblum finally located a paper cutout of Picasso's dog Klipper, done when the artist was a boy of 12 or 13 in Spain. Both Manet and Renoir painted a Japanese Chin name Tama (which means jewel in Japanese) in their own inimitable styles. The dog was brought back from the Far East by a French orientalist, who commissioned the two great French Impressionists to paint a portrait of his beloved companion. Duane Hansen's works resemble funerary statues with everyone frozen in time. A sculpture of his own beagle was cast after the dog died. Roy Lichtenstein's comic strip dog says "Grr." Amos, Andy Warhol's pet dachshund and constant companion, was immortalized by the artist. About his canine publishing venture, Rosenblum says, "I've never been involved with anything so offbeat in my life. I'll be giving lectures and gallery talks on the book, which I love to do. This book is a good balance to squaredom."

Married and the father of two, Rosenblum has no dogs of his own, but "frequently dog-sits" for friends. "After a few days the kids have gotten bored, and I'm less enchanted with a midnight walk four times around the block, so I'm happy to give them back. But who really doesn't like dogs?" □

15

DOG'S BEST FRIEND

William Wegman gets his paws on Polaroid film— how one man shot his dogs for art.

BY AMEI WELSH CORGI

F ay emerges from red foil, like a giant canine bonbon. She balances gracefully on an ironing board. Fay again, sharing the spotlight with a woman named Andrea and forming a double portrait of two attractive females. For Fay, this is all in a day's work—she is a famous artist's model. Fay Ray, named after King Kong's sidekick, is the striking Weimaraner who is prominently featured in William Wegman's latest photographic work.

Wegman has been active since the late sixties and is known for a wide range of work in various media, including drawing, painting, video and photography (through the back door, as he says). All his artistic expression is informed by humor. His earliest video efforts included film of his first canine companion, another Weimaraner named Man Ray. Ray was not originally intended to be the subject of Wegman's work, but the irresistible young dog had a way of ingratiating himself into the picture. He was Wegman's constant companion, and when the lively animal began to interfere with the day's work, Wegman tried tying him up in a corner of the studio. The dog expressed his loud displeasure with this arrangement. To maintain his sanity, and a quiet studio, Wegman had to devise a way to include the dog in his work. He began to photograph and film Ray in a number of situations suggested by the dog's own nature and instinctual behavior. That is why we find Ray chewing on a microphone in one of the early videos, Reel 1. Photographs of the dog would be altered or enhanced with painted elements to create images that could not be captured with film alone. One early portrait of Ray showed the dog with painted-on ears and whiskers. The result was a catlike photo

called "Ray Cat." Other examples of this technique included "Man Ray," with the dog sporting the painted beard and spectacles of his artist namesake, and "Noble Dog—Paint by Numbers," in which a photo of the dog was outlined and shaded to make it look like a painting created from a kit. As Ray grew older and better trained, Wegman created more complicated situations for him to enact and began to explore the graceful shapes and poses the dog's body could achieve.

Ray enjoyed the attention hugely and became a very competent and willing model. Wegman called the dog and himself "co-conspirators" because Ray viewed their work as a cooperative arrangement—an exchange of service for the reward of attention and friendship. When Wegman worked on his own to explore his drawing ability, Ray resented the interruptions in their work and would stalk into the studio, glare at Wegman and sulk. Wegman got the message, and resumed his work with Ray.

In the late seventies, Wegman had to confront the fact that his canine friend had grown older, his body heavier and less graceful than in its younger days. As Wegman knew, this was a problem inherent in every long relationship between artist and model. Wegman injected new vitality into their working day by exploring the possibility of draping his aging model with materials to create new forms and new situations to conceal the bulkiness of his body. He wished to draw the eye away from the dog's shape and capture the humor of bizarre situations created through the use of costumes and props. Ray's past experience as a model made it easy for him to cooperate in these new, more complicated photos.

In 1978, Wegman was invited by the Polaroid Corporation to use its new, large-format camera. The equipment enabled Wegman to create 20-x-24-inch instant-

Fay and William Wegman. It's all in a day's work.

KATLEEN STERCK

Barkarat

AT THE SERVICE OF BEST-IN-SHOW WINNERS, CELEBRITIES, COMPANIONS AND MERE PAMPERED PETS SINCE 1776.

Of all the

Art

color photos. Each image was an original, and the results could be seen 85 seconds after the photo was taken. The technique let Wegman alter his shot, the model or the prop elements to make changes that would eventually result in a single image that satisfied him. Typically, he would take up to twenty shots before he came upon the combination that would be the final image. This method proved especially well suited to the photos he had begun to take of Ray. The large-format Polaroids of Ray became perhaps the best-known facet of Wegman's work.

Favorite images of Ray included "Airedale," a photo of the dog wrapped in gold Christmas tinsel; "Frog," Ray wearing swimming flippers and Ping-Pong-ball eyes; "Brooke," Ray in designer jeans; and "Baby Magic," Ray covered in baby powder standing next to a container of Baby Magic talc. Memorable images from this series were collected in *Man's Best Friend*, a paperback published by Harry N. Abrams in 1982.

Sadly, the dog who inspired Wegman did not live to see himself immortalized between book covers. Ray developed cancer and died at eleven and a half before work on the book was completed. The

book was dedicated to him, and to the famous human artist for whom he had been named and who died in 1976. Both Man Rays contributed to Wegman's artistic sensibility; both were instrumental in the ultimate creation of the book.

After the dog's death, Wegman returned to drawing and painting and began to photograph non-canine subjects. His work was exhibited at six major museums around the country. "I think they [called] it a midcareer retrospective," said Wegman. "It has a nice summary quality. Man Ray had just died, so it was really his retrospective. And it was a nice way of putting a bracket around the period. I was sad to lose Ray, but it was liberating in a way. I felt it was time to try other things."

A show of new work soon after Ray's death failed to get the same attention as previous shows. One reviewer said, "I miss the dog." Wegman replied, "Likewise."

Wegman owned two other dogs after Ray. One died and the other was stolen. He didn't plan on having another Weimaraner. But after a lecture in Memphis several years ago, he met a woman in the audience who happened to be a breeder of Weimaraners. "I went to

see the litter," Wegman said, "but I told her I just wasn't ready. Then I got on the plane, and it was like a perfume ad—I couldn't get one dog's face out of my mind." He called the breeder and asked her to send the dog, called Cinnamon Girl, the next day. He renamed the dog Fay (the "Ray" is understood). After she had become familiar with her new surroundings, Wegman began to train his new model.

He soon discovered that the two Weimaraners were very different in tem-

will hold a difficult pose in part for the praise she receives, but even more because she knows it's her job. Fay is also a more aesthetically interesting model, and Wegman does not need to rely as heavily on the humorous props and situations that were the hallmarks of his earlier work.

Wegman is surprised by the occasional

Fay: left to right,
Hatched; Fay on Board,
Fay and Andrea.

perament as well as appearance. Man Ray was strong and masculine, Fay more delicate and graceful. For Man Ray, modeling was a game, and Wegman had used the dog's sense of play to dress him as other animals. Fay, more compliant, poses because Wegman wants her to. She

complaints about his work with the canine models. People unfamiliar with the gentle ways in which he coaxes his subjects into posing for the camera feel that he may be treating the animals cruelly when he dresses them in costumes or positions them with props. A more understanding response to the dynamics in Wegman's studio was expressed by Sanford Schwartz in a piece in *The New York Review of Books*. For the dog, he guessed, the work is "a stretched-out version of the crazed and blissful moment in a dog's life when his master picks up his lead, the metal clasp clinks, and he realizes that he's going to be taken for a walk."

Both Fay and Ray were motivated by a sense of professionalism, but more than that, by keen pleasure in their work. Modeling, and the recognition and praise it afforded them, was a natural high. They knew they were special, and their pride is visible in the photographs. That is why Ray permitted Wegman to cover him in yarn or flowers, and why Fay was content to be encased in foil or balance precariously on an ironing board. The dogs willingly made sacrifices for their art, but pride in a job well done is the ultimate gratification. □

19

DONNACAIRN
NEW YORK

funfur

A Deb and Her Dog

Yo!…What's all the fuss about Cornelia Guest and Sylvester Stallone? Corny and Sly, Sly and Corny?… The *real* love affair is between Cornelia and *Lyle,* her West Highland white terrier. Not long ago, gossip hounds were burning up the phone lines with reports about Cornelia's tearful time. Was she crying over Sly? The *real* inside poop is that Lyle managed to wander away from his and Cornelia's plush Beverly Hills digs. The precious pooch was missing for two weeks and Cornelia's eyes weren't dry for a single moment until he returned! We just love a happy ending….

Photographed by **SILBERSTEIN**

21

© 1987 SPANGLED CAT FOUNDATION

Living Room Leopards

The exotically spotted wildcat stalked his prey and leaped...onto the sofa! You see, the California Spangled Cat, which retains the dramatic spotted coat of a wildcat, is actually an affectionate breed of domestic cat. The breed was called "leopards for your living room" when a pair of these rare cats was featured as the exclusive "his 'n' hers" gift, at $1,400 each, in the 1986 Neiman-Marcus Christmas catalog. Paul Casey, a Hollywood scriptwriter who devoted fifteen years to developing the rare breed, is kept busy filling all the orders. Since the catalog was issued, the price has gone even higher, but the demand for these dotted dazzlers continues. They say a cat can't change his spots—and that's just fine with Casey!

Bone Appétit

Share your favorite snack with your people. Throw the folks a bone! They're sure to enjoy them—they're made of chocolate. Popular chocolate designs include the "Cats at Play" series featuring cats embossed on mint, milk or dark chocolate; "Sweet Silhouettes," with its popular dog breeds embossed on rounds of chocolate, paw prints and "Best-in-Show" rosettes. All chocolates are wrapped in gold, silver or red foil; they make the perfect gift for people, who are so often hard to please.

BRUCE PLOTKIN

Cat Boxes

This cat box has her *own* kitty litter—two delightful kitten boxes. These hand-carved beauties can be used to store your treasures, catnip treats or even a mouse for a rainy day.

Heavy Petting

Here's the rub. Until now, plump pooches, fat cats and other pets suffering signs of stress were denied the benefits offered to humans at health spas. The Argyle Fountain Spa in Argyle, Texas, has changed all that. Four-legged patrons may accompany their two-legged companions to a variety of healthy activities. Pets, along with people, are treated to daily exercise, therapeutic baths and grooming options, which include facials and massages. Dog tired? Time to flea? Might be time to make a reservation.

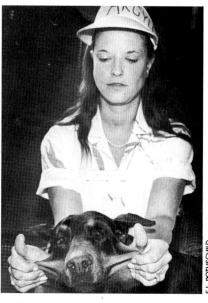

S.L. ROTHSCHILD

funfur

W e canines and felines have a deep appreciation of art, especially when it features our favorite subject matter—ourselves! Dogs will surely enjoy a visit to The Dog Museum of America. Aside from the fact that it may be the only museum that welcomes us, it may well be the only one that will interest us. In addition to its distinguished collection, the museum offers a continuing program of timely exhibits on art and other matters of cultural interest to dogdom. It has a new home in Saint Louis, so stop and visit when you're there with your people.

Several art galleries both in the United States and abroad specialize in canine and feline subjects. William Secord Fine Arts in New York City and The Sara Davenport Gallery in London are two that specialize in animal paintings, prints and decorative objects. Both galleries maintain files of their customers' breed preferences and notify them of any new items of interest.

Jay Johnson's America's Folk Heritage Gallery in New York City features contemporary works that retain the robust, primitive flavor of folk art. Many animals are depicted in their collections, but the works featuring felines and canines are, needless to say, especially charming.

Art for the Furry Masses

Sweet Smell of Success

Martine, an apricot toy poodle who, with her companion, Lisa Gilford, owns a fashionable New York City pet shop and grooming salon called Le Chien, wouldn't dream of leaving the house without her cultured-pearl necklace, her diamond pavé heart on a gold chain or a spritz of her favorite fragrance. Martine, a perfume blended from jasmine and tuberose, was designed just for her. A companion cologne called Christophe for male dogs (wild flowers, sandalwood and bergamot) is also available. Stop in to sample the scents, and see the special array of jewels, clothes and accessories that Martine has selected.

BRUCE PLOTKIN

funfur

BRUCE PLOTKIN

Stamp of Approval

*Roll over Fido, a row of cats, or a
parade of paw prints. These novel rubber-
stamp rollers are called Wonder Wheels.™
The roller can leave your mark on
anything you choose, from purrsonal
notes to furvorite people!*

Amaruffo di Rex

BRUCE PLOTKIN

GAY LINDSAY

Designs for Living

Ché, a Siamese cat who shares his opulent Central Park West apartment with his people, recently had the pleasure of working with Carl D'Aquino and Geo. Wm. Humphreys, Jr., on the design of his new home. D'Aquino and Humphreys, a pair of young designers worth watching, consulted with Ché and other members of the family to learn of any particular needs before creating a room especially suited to their feline client. The designers created an oak-paneled library with a spectacular view of Central Park for the cat, who takes great pleasure in gazing at the park's flora and fauna. Ché was provided with a tapestry-covered ottoman that affords him an excellent view of the park and is also a perfect spot for one of his many daily naps. The ottoman is large enough for Ché to stretch out comfortably, while providing his people with ample room on which to rest their feet. The tapestry fabric is from Brunschwig et Fils, and the design offers Ché a dense texture he can dig his claws into without wreaking undue damage.

S. CODI

She's a Real Doll

"Here's Barbie." Except that this time, she's a real dog! The perfect playmate for puppies, "Barbie Dog" is only one of several canine creations from Washington artist Suzanne Codi. Other specialties are "Dalmangels"—Dalmation Angel ornaments for your Christmas tree.

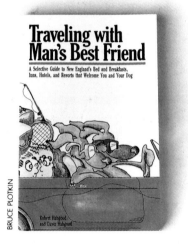

BRUCE PLOTKIN

Dog Gone

Traveling with Man's Best Friend *may be viewed as a "Fodor's for Fido." There are currently three travel guides in the series: California (this one includes Oregon and Washington); New England; the Eastern seaboard. The books are a selective guide to the bed-and-breakfasts, inns and hotels that welcome you just as warmly as they do your people.*

Perpetual Care

The Living Free Animal Shelter in Mountain Center, California, offers a unique form of assurance to animals: Should their human companions pass on or become unable to provide them with adequate care, the animals will be looked after lovingly. This orphanage for cats and dogs is a non-profit organization sustained by donations or by membership in a continuing-care program. For more information, contact the shelter.

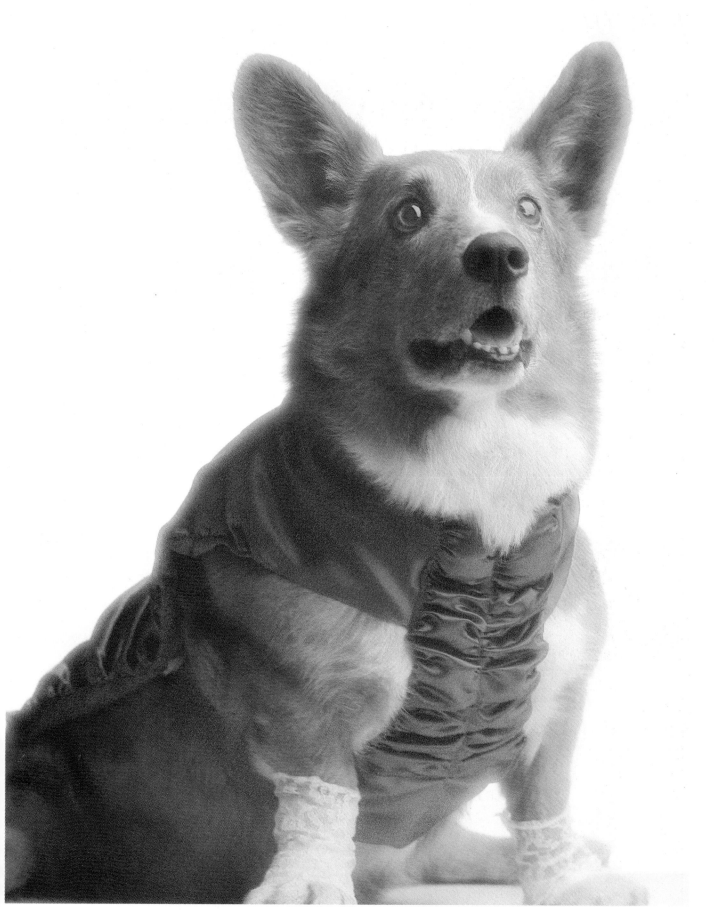

GIORGIO ARFMANI

funfur

Plush Mush

*Trophée Revillon is an annual
international dog sled race.
Inaugurated in 1987, the race
will be hosted in alternating years
by an American and a European
ski resort. It is sponsored by the
world-renowned furriers, Revillon,
under the auspices of the International Sled Dog Racing
Association. While many jet-set
celebrities attend the race, the
real stars are the sled dogs, who
are fêted with French Champagne
at the finish line.*

BRUCE PLOTKIN

Proxy Pets

Are you an only dog or cat in need
of animal companionship? Too
greedy to share your meals and toys
with another animal? Then try a
tape. Creative Programming has
produced two videotape cassettes
that provide "the full, rich experience of owning your own dog (or
cat) without the mess and inconven-
ience of the real thing." *Video Dog*
or *Video Cat* is the perfect gift
idea for that lazy but pet-loving
person on your holiday gift list!

Celebrity Pet Priorities

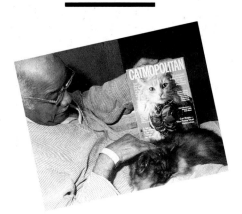

Professional pet models and actors make time for a "pet project"—participa-
tion in a pet-therapy program to aid disabled veterans. Chickie, a gray
Persian cat who appeared in *Catmopolitan*, and Goldie, a Chihuahua who
was featured in *Dogue*, are only two of the many celebrities who take part in
the non-profit program sponsored by the Center for Pet Therapy. The
program, organized by renowned animal-trainer Bashkim Dibra of
Fieldston Pets in New York City, has been successful in helping veterans
reduce stress, improve socialization, increase self-confidence and even
lower blood pressure. And all from just a hug....

In the Swim

Canadian sea dogs look forward to the Annual Dog Swim at the Canadian National Exhibition. The event, in which a dog swims behind a rowboat peopled by his or her companion (and partner in the race), is a canine favorite. Competing in classes that correspond to weight or breed, the dogs enjoy their moment in the sun (no matter how wet it might be). The event is sponsored by Ralston Purina of Canada.

BRUCE PLOTKIN

The Best Little Cat House

The elegant Palladian-style home is built to classical proportions . . . from cardboard. Don't let the materials fool you— this is a dramatic design that would please the most discriminating feline occupant. The design features columns, arches, sculptures and other architectural elements executed in engraved patterns on this light and fanciful cat house. On the matte silver roof is a charming engraving of a cat. This "cat on a hot tin roof" points to the convenient handle that helps lift the house off a concealed litter box, for easy disposal.

BRUCE PLOTKIN

Get a Head

Cuddly lapdogs or delicate cats can now inspire fear and respect from all. The Dobermask is a large foam-rubber mask of a Doberman pinscher's head. You slip it on and it instantly provides even the most diminutive pet with a fiercely threatening aspect. The mask is a product of Slycraft, whose motto is: "Solve a problem that doesn't exist with a product that doesn't work."

funfur

COURTESY OF MORRIS ANIMAL FOUNDATION

Golden Girl's Generosity

Betty White, actress and longtime animal lover, is national spokesperson for the Morris Animal Foundation. A former president of the organization, Ms. White has been active in preparations for the Foundation's fortieth-anniversary year. She has made numerous appearances to publicize the work of the group in its efforts to provide better health for all companion animals (dogs, cats, horses and zoo animals). The Morris Animal Foundation funds research in health problems that plague these animals; through its work, the organization has helped combat disease and fostered good health and nutrition practices. The non-profit organization needs your help. Please send a tax-deductible donation, or contact them for more information.

Hold That Leopard

Piero Fornasetti is a multitalented artist from Milan, Italy. Painter, sculptor, interior decorator, printer of art books, designer of stage sets, costumes and exhibitions, he has produced more than 11,000 decorative articles. We are particularly taken with his representation of a leopard stalking across a chest of drawers.

Cavalier Roehm (*fashion designer*): Doggie Brown's Gourmet Bones—*"They're dipped in carob or yogurt, so they can taste sinfully like chocolate, but they're good for you. And not dreadfully fattening, either."*

ALEX BOIES

Debbie Hairy (*singer*): Haute Feline Gourmet Snacks for Cats—*"I enjoy the amusing little fish shapes and the authentic tuna flavor."*

Katleen Turner (*actress*): Jackie's Cat Snacks—*"The Hollywood variety is my favorite. It combines shrimp, clam and tuna, and I just love seafood."*

Karl Dogerfeld

Faux Fourrures

Sphynx Fifth Avenue

EXACT FUR COLOR

What you see here is Colorpurrinting. The shade that seems to disappear into your fur identifies your Exact Fur Color family and the one fur shade that matches your furtone exactly. In just five minutes it will change the way you choose fur enhancers forever.

PURRSCR

EXACT FUR CARE

ience has linked shedding to a natural
ocess which eliminates old, dead fur.
ur Ball Preventor works to eliminate dan-
erous fur balls from your system. You
n't stop shedding. But Fur Ball Preventor
elps prevent a dangerous and painful fur
uild-up before it begins.

...Fluff Report...
Superior New Formula....Advanced Fur Ball Protection!

PURRSCRIPTIVES

FURBALL

PREVENTOR

PTIVES

funfur

© 1988 GINA BILANDER

Run for Your Life

The sleek, fast greyhound is the premier dog at racetracks all over the country. But after the race is run and won, when the dogs grow too slow to compete, most of them are destroyed. Many never live to see their second birthday. Several kind humans have set up organizations to rescue these greyhounds. One group is called Greyhound Friends, and its founder, Louise Coleman, cares for about thirty-five dogs while suitable adoptive homes are being located. Open your heart, and home, to a winner.

Best Bytes

Thomas J. Watson III, son and grandson of the men who brought you IBM, has more important concerns on his mind than the family business: canine nutrition and real meat flavor. The only bytes on his agenda are the ones that go into our mouths. He and his partner, James Lucchesi, have developed a meat-flavored gravy called FYDO (an acronym for For Your Dog Only). It was specially formulated by veterinarians to make dog food tastier, and to add essential nutrients that may be missing from your diet.

All in the Family

Mario Buatta, "the Prince of Chintz," shares his home with many dogs, all of them inanimate. The famed interior designer has adorned his "ancestral digs" with portraits of his "family" members, all of them dogs (in the literal sense, if we can believe what we see in the paintings). The eighteenth- and nineteenth-century oil paintings include "the Boxer Rebellion, as painted by a painter to the Queen in 1902; my brother and I—I was the black sheep in the family; my paternal grandfather, the Postmaster General; and my maternal grandfather, the Confederate General." We *do* notice a certain family resemblance. I guess that's why dogs have always felt at home with Buatta and his designs....

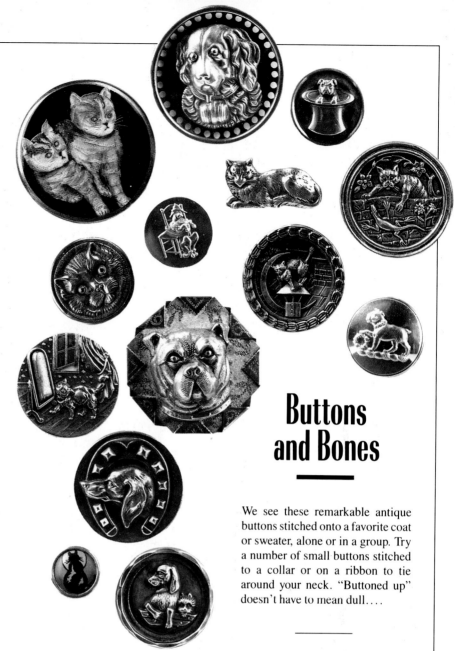

Neat Feat Treat

At last! Someone has designed a gumball machine especially for dogs! The "Yuppy Puppy Doggy Treet" dispenser looks just like an antique gumball machine—only this time no pennies are required. Just press on the bone-shaped lever for a tasty treat! Jealous kittens may not have long to wait—a kitty-treat machine is planned.

Buttons and Bones

We see these remarkable antique buttons stitched onto a favorite coat or sweater, alone or in a group. Try a number of small buttons stitched to a collar or on a ribbon to tie around your neck. "Buttoned up" doesn't have to mean dull....

BRUCE PLOTKIN

Disney Goes to the Dogs

Poor Walt never suspected the fate that lay in store. Disney has finally gone to the dogs, and you can get in on the action! Canines are still denied entry to Disneyland and Disney World (though they do provide kennels where we can wait for our people in comfort). However, the gift shops in the theme parks now carry a red turtleneck sweater with a satin appliqué of Pluto on the back.

Crafty animals may choose to try their paws at knitting a Disney-design sweater of their own, though you may find it easier to convince your people to do it for you. *The Disney Book of Knitting,* by Melinda Coss and Debby Robinson (St. Martin's Press), will provide complete instructions on how to knit your favorite Disney characters. The rest is up to you.

Frequent Fliers

Some four-legged travelers cross the ocean with a frequency that equals or exceeds that of the most active members of the human jet set. This "pet set" includes socialite Pumpkin Mathews, a four-pound, champagne-colored toy poodle who, accompanied by her people, jets on the Concorde between her homes in New York City and St. Tropez. Pumpkin never travels without her Louis Vuitton bag, a supply of designer scarves and her autograph book (for the signatures of fellow celebrities she's met on board).

A far less enthusiastic feline traveler named Felix reluctantly, and unexpectedly, racked up 179,189 miles on 64 Pan Am flights during a 29-day period. Felix, who lives with Janice, William and Nadine Kubecki, was returning to California from Frankfurt, Germany, where her family was stationed. She escaped from her carrier in the baggage compartment of the plane and was declared missing until she emerged, safe but confused and exhausted, 29 days later at the London airport. The high-flying cat had traveled to twelve countries! Her reunion with her family after her first-class arrival home was a media event. In recognition of her newly acquired frequent-flier status, she was presented with a pair of round-trip first-class tickets to any country in the world serviced by Pan Am. Felix quickly turned the tickets over to the Kubeckis. She'd had more than enough flying for a while....

LOS ANGELES TIMES PHOTO

And a Happy New Year

BRUCE PLOTKIN

Meowy Chrismouse is a 7-inch, 45-rpm record of popular feline Christmas songs purrformed by the famous Tabbynacle Choir. Side one features the rousing "Caterwaul of the Bells," with the unfurgettable choir accompanied by the Fleaharmonic Orchestra. The purrformance was recorded live at the Meowtropolitan Opera House. Side two includes the hair-raising "Meowy Chrismouse Medley," which combines the holiday favorites "O Chrismouse Tree," "Alleycats We've Heard on High," "We Three Cats from Orient Way," "O Come All Ye Felines" and "We Wish You a Meowy Chrismouse."

BRUCE PLOTKIN

Beware of Cat... and Dog

These amusing signs in French admonish the reader to "Beware lunatic cat" or "Beware bizarre dog." What a wonderful idea. We're buying them for all our friends!

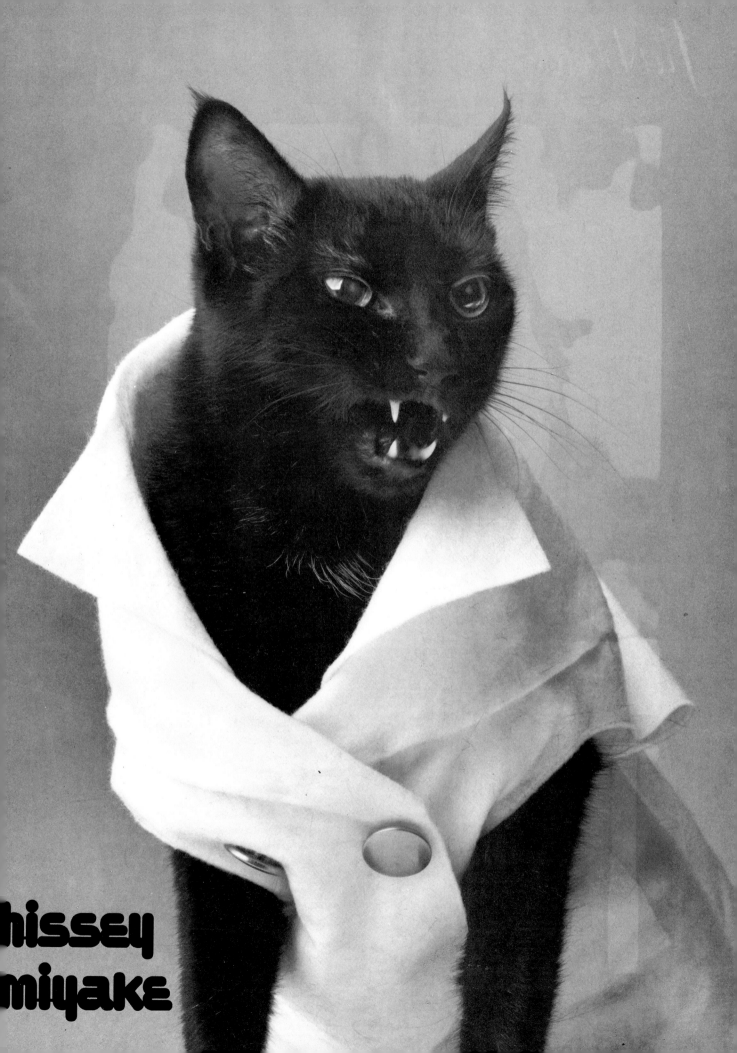

hissey miyake

flashback

Benji

Thirteen years ago, the silver screen was treated to a new kind of hero. Like many other leading men, he was handsome and strong—but he was certainly not silent. With his first bark, Benji endeared himself to the entire four-legged (*and* two-legged) population. In 1975, the film *Benji* was released. Its success, and that of Benji himself as a new American hero, led to *For the Love of Benji* in 1977. Benji was in great demand as a television star as well; 1977 also marked his debut on the small screen in "The Phenomenon of Benji."

Today, after two additional films, three more television specials and a television live-action series, Benji has achieved international fame. He is a superstar in Japan and Australia, as well as in the United States. His travels to promote his various projects have taken him to France, Switzerland, Italy, Greece, Germany, Canada, Puerto Rico, South America, Hawaii and the Far East. He was the second animal to be inducted into the American Humane Society's Animal Actors Hall of Fame (Lassie was the first). He has twice received the American Guild of Variety Artists' Georgie Award as the Top Animal Entertainer of the Year.

His motion picture theme song, "I Feel Love," won a Golden Globe award and was nominated for an Academy Award. Along with such stars as John Wayne and Bob Hope, he was voted one of the ten most popular performers in the United States by the Performer Q survey. Yet, through all his fortune and fame, he remains down to earth and unaffected, living unpretentiously in a ranch-style home in a Los Angeles suburb. The embodiment worldwide of warmth and love, Benji is the free world's most huggable hero.

Photograph by JOE CAMP

The Red Pet Collar.
Now Available In Water Bowls.

Thanks to Spaniel, anyplace you like to eat can also be a convenient place to shop. Our Spring Cat-a-log includes the latest designs from Ruff Lauren, Calvin Klaw, Adrienne Vittadogi, Hiss Clawborne and others. To receive your copy for just 3 bones, or 3 mice, simply call (toll-free) 1-800-ANI-MALS and ask for the catalog for four-legged friends.

Spaniel

The Fur Is

Yves Saint Bernard has bee[n]

the master of French fashion f[or]

more than a decade. His dog da[ys]

may be over. Christian Lacla[u]

the new kitten in tow[n]

believes that a cat can look [at]

a king...and purrha[ps]

overthrow him. EDMU[N]

WHIPPET sniffs o[ut]

the real story from Pa[ris]

Flying

He was the undisputed king of roll-over-and-play-dead fashion.

Where is Yves Saint Bernard? There was a time, not so long ago, that he was everywhere. *Dog's Wear Daily (DWD)*, the bible of the pet fashion industry, breathlessly noted every new fashion trend that emerged from his doghouse. The rest of the fashion press grabbed the bone and ran with it. Every issue of *Dogue* and *Harpurr's Bazaar* heralded his latest fashion dogma. Fashion hounds devoured his message. Well-heeled canines and the doggies who lunch followed his every fashion command. He was the undisputed king of roll-over-and-play-dead fashion. And then he was gone.

Pawing through the pages of their favorite periodicals, fashion hounds could find no trace of their beloved Saint Bernard. The pages, and covers, were now filled with stories about the new kitten in town. A crazy cat named Christian Laclaw was snatching all the headlines with news about his extravagant, fanciful clothes. "Dress to excess" was the new fashion catcall.

What had become of Saint Bernard? Too much power, thought some. The lack of competition had made him fat and lazy, and his designs reflected his indifference. He had been known for creating innovative new trends; now he turned out dumb dog coats and dresses. Several pet patrons were heard to remark that they already had those clothes in their closets, and craved something new. Saint Bernard failed to recognize that the dog had had his day. Cats were growing in popularity and now outnumbered dogs in most American homes.

Felines were more independent than dogs and demanded exciting new clothes to herald their new prominence. They were sexier and more mysterious than dogs and craved a look all their own. They would not submit to Saint Bernard's dull new copycat designs. Cats called out for a new fashion leader who could catapult to the top. Laclaw was in the catbird seat.

The cat tales began to fly. Anna Winpurr, the new editor of *MG (Mouse and Garden)*, expanded the focus of her redesigned magazine to include several of Laclaw's more outrageous feline designs. This led some readers to question whether the "G" in "MG" referred to "garment." John Fairpuppy, the all-powerful publisher of *DWD*, felt that Saint Bernard had grown stale and embraced the wildcat designs of Laclaw in the pages of his widely read periodical. Saint Bernard's business partner, Poodle Bergé, who is known for his snappy temper, lifted his leg to Fairpuppy at a party, and the dogfight was on. Saint Bernard was relegated to the position of "non-dog" in the pages of *DWD*, an unhappy fate suffered by only one other top designer, Geoffrey Bone. The late Hebe Dogsay, who had been the influential fashion editor of *The International Hairy Tribune*, joined in the fracas with her widely published catty remark, "We lost Saint Bernard," as though the great dog were dead.

Together Fairpuppy and Dogsay, two movers and shakers in the furry world of fashion, conspired to tiptoe around the sleeping giant and crown a new head of fashion before Saint Bernard could awaken. Even now Laclaw's influence is growing by leaps and bounds, and the fashion hounds are sitting up and taking notice.

In a recent interview, when questioned about the ongoing battle for fashion leadership, Laclaw remarked coyly, "Let sleeping dogs lie. I just take catnaps." And with that, he stretched his paws and sharpened his claws for the next round of the fashion fight. The King is dead. Long live the King.

_____

A black-and-white issue: Saint Bernard's somber harlequin design, *right,* faces off Laclaw's fanciful milkmaid, *opposite page.*

"Dress to excess"
was the new fashion catcall

Box Car Willie Reagan shares the chair with Millie Bush at the Republican Pet Fête.
Blazer Lugar and Baby Bleep Bentley look on.

Democratic Dog party hosted by Peppi Pepper.

The pretty pink town house, a short distance from the White House on Washington's Pennsylvania Avenue, looks just like any other carefully restored Georgetown residence. In a neighborhood famous for its Federal architecture, this small pink brick building, with large windows offering a glimpse of the parlor floor, is no exception. It's just the kind of house in which your congressman or senator might live. A charming home in a desirable neighborhood...but this one has gone to the dogs.

That's right. The elegant facade of the building is perfectly in keeping with the elite atmosphere found within this preferred meeting place for Washington's power pets—the Bone Jour Café. This is where the city powermongers (or was that *mongrels*?) gravitate to get away from the dog-eat-dog power whirl of Washington or to exchange the latest inside poop on what's happening in the country's capital.

It was here at Bone Jour that many of the city's movers and shakers discussed the Capital Canine Follies over a snack of Veggie Men (thus starting the rumor that they were a man-eating bunch). This was also the place where First Dog Rex Reagan found his personalized ceramic dish and matching hand-painted tile placemat, prompting his companion, First Lady Nancy Reagan, to dash off a note on White House stationery: "I'm sure little Rex will enjoy mealtime more in his personalized ceramic bowl." The late C. Fred Bush, renowned canine author, statesman and esteemed companion of George and Barbara Bush, was especially fond of Bone Jour's Scone Bones. The Café has long enjoyed a reputation for catering to the city's power pooches and was recently chosen as the site for the National Convention of Canine Companions to the Candidates.

In keeping with the nation's traditional two-party system, Democrat and Republican canines caucused in separate but equal parties held in the Café's private upstairs meeting rooms.

The Republican fête was hosted by Box Car Willie Reagan, chairman of the Republican Pet National Committee. Willie, as he is known to his cronies in the D.C. power hierarchy, lives with Maureen Reagan. The political bug seems to have bitten the entire Reagan family. Maureen herself was a co-chairperson of the Republican National Committee. Her father, Ronald Reagan, was President of the United States; his wife, Nancy Reagan, was First Lady. But, more important, their companion, Rex Reagan, was the nation's First Dog.

THE TWO-PARTY SYSTEM

GAIL SHEDDY
reports on the bi-partisan fun

Willie's fellow committee members included Mildred (Millie) Bush, who shared the chair with Willie (literally). Millie resides with George and Barbara Bush and is a familiar figure among the political dog set. Baby Bleep Bentley, the companion of Maryland Congresswoman Helen Bentley, and Blazer Lugar, who shares digs with Indiana Senator Richard Lugar, rounded out the Republican Committee.

Willie arranged for an elegant, and topical, table to be set for his guests. The floral centerpiece, in red, white and blue, was adorned with flags, which also appeared on the silver bowls found at each place setting. The bowls contained the famous G.O.P.–D.O.G. cookies cut in the shape of an elephant, and a rubber effigy of Mikhail Gorbachev that squeaked when chewed. Just what the power barkers discussed at the party must remain confidential, but the presence of a photojournalist whose work appears in *The Washington Post* seemed to confirm the group's reputation as major media hounds.

The Democratic dogs planned a smaller party. Their gathering, hosted by chairman Peppi Pepper (who resides with Florida Congressman Claude Pepper), included Wolfie Schroeder (who spends his time with Colorado Congresswoman Pat Schroeder) and Junket Aspin (companion to Wisconsin Congressman Les Aspin). Junket, whose energetic campaign efforts made her a legend back in Wisconsin, wore a striking red and orange T-shirt silkscreened with her name and image. She has generously distributed many of these shirts to members of her constituency back home. The other members of her committee were offered shirts, too, but respectfully declined.

The Democratic Dogs Party set a splendid table featuring red, white and blue tissue-paper balls, flags and silver bowls containing the Yellow Dog Democrat Dog Bones, which have become the Party's favorite. Margaret Thatcher chew toys adorned each place setting. The napkins were trimmed with the Party's mascot, the donkey. Once again, the decisions reached at the meeting are classified information, but one reporter's dispatch said his eavesdropping had convinced him it was mostly "ambassadoggerel."

The inner circle of Washington's power pups has thus far commented only that both parties were a social and culinary success. The political ramifications of the pet powwows remain to be seen, but one thing was made perfectly clear. No bones about it—Washington is going to the dogs. □

THE JET SET'S PET VET

What do Tyler Kissinger, Peaches Petrie, Cesare Scavullo, Martini Tiegs and Spike Rivers have in common? Well, in addition to the great distinction of being canine or feline and of sharing family life with a prominent personality, this particular group was recently assembled in the waiting room of one of New York's premier veterinarians, Dr. Lewis Berman of the Park East Animal Hospital. One sunny morning found the five rubbing elbows, all twenty of them, with several other animals in Dr. Berman's sumptuously appointed townhouse offices.

I heaved an inner woof of relief: I was there to interview the doctor in my professional role as *Vanity Fur* reporter. I thanked my lucky Dog Star that no poking, no prodding, no surprises in the examining room were in store for me. I was early for my appointment and chewed nervously on a claw, reliving an early medical trauma that still haunts me. Years before, I was given a rabies shot with no warning whatsoever. I had howled in outrage and to this day never completely trust anyone in white. Pawing nervously through a copy of *New Yorkie* magazine, I wondered how Dr. Berman's patients managed to remain so calm. *They* were here for treatment, while I was merely going to observe the doctor on a typical office day. Why did they seem so relaxed? What was the doctor's secret?

Photographed by BRUCE PLOTKIN

MIKE HAMILL visits with Dr. Lewis Berman, who cures what ails them.

erhaps, I reflected, the unique decor contributed to their sense of well-being. A handsome example of post-modern design, the environment has been created with animal comfort and safety foremost in mind. The floors are made of a special crushed marble mixture that is not slippery beneath our paws. It is nonporous and simple to clean and disinfect. The walls are painted with zolatone, whose trendy spattered appearance masks wear and tear and is easily washed clean. The art, too, reflects a sensitive awareness of animal subjects and features, among other works, an Alex Katz portrait of a Skye terrier, a gift to the doctor from a grateful patient.

One by one, the doctor called in his patients. Next to me sat a handsome Persian cat reading a copy of *No Bad Dogs* with a highly skeptical expression. Apologizing for the intrusion, I introduced myself and asked, "How do you explain Dr. Berman's popularity with New York's four-footed population?"

"My dear fellow," she exclaimed, "he is a purrfectly wonderful human being, kind and caring, and an equally fine vet."

When he had attended to all his patients, the doctor strode in and extended a friendly hand to my waiting paw. He suggested we start with a tour of the offices, and off we went.

The two main-floor examining rooms featured glass-block walls, which permit light to enter without sacrificing patient privacy. The decorative etched-glass doors achieve the same effect. I appreciated this concern for our modesty, which is so often neglected. For all its handsome decor, however, the office is highly functional. The facility features such state-of-the-art medical equipment as an X-ray machine that permits automatic processing in a two-and-a-half-minute cycle. This means that X-rays can be taken and viewed in the course of a few minutes, to aid quickly in the diagnosis of painful or potentially dangerous ailments.

An intensive-care unit on the second floor features a controlled environment for recuperating patients and can be programmed to provide a dry, heated or humid environment, as required. If necessary, oxygen can be administered here. Basic laboratory procedures like urinalysis and heartworm testing are also conducted at the office to save time and ensure accuracy. The on-site operating room contains the very latest equipment in veterinary medicine.

The tour was impressive; it was easy to see why Manhattan's in-the-know pet circle made its way to Dr. Berman's office. The combination of his old-fashioned kindness and concern and the modern technical equipment in his office was more than enough explanation. How, I asked him, did he enjoy his reputation as the jet set's pet vet?

He pondered briefly and replied, "I don't like being called the society vet, if being the society vet means that you socialize with them. I don't run into them socially. People like Pat Buckley, Nancy Kissinger, Lauren Bacall and Cheryl Tiegs—these and other celebrities want the best for their pets. We give everyone the best care; that's why they come here."

And Dr. Berman means *everyone*.

For every celebrity pet examined, he also sees pets whose family names are not household words, animals much like you and me, and like the stray cats brought into his office by Sister Maureen of the Sisters of Mercy in the Bronx. These cats, often suffering with worms and fleas, are given the same care and concern as his other patients. Once restored to health, they are neutered and offered for adoption. Many go home as companions to other patients. Indeed, celebrity clients comprise only a handful of the patients treated by Dr. Berman and his associates, Dr. Gene Solomon, Dr. Amy Attas, and their technician, Dale Mitchell.

Many of his clients call from all over the country for advice and reassurance. Lily Tomlin, for example, became a client when she starred on Broadway, but still calls for advice from her home in California. Lauren Bacall toured the country with her Cavalier King Charles spaniel which had grown old and sickly. Dr. Berman arranged for vets in each of her touring cities to monitor the dog's health. Henry Kissinger once spent the entire day conducting his affairs from Dr. Berman's office while awaiting the outcome of his dog Tyler's operation. Businessman "Ace" Greenberg of Bear Stearns, who is devoted to his dog, calls the doctor's office during the middle of the trading day for veterinary advice. The doctor takes these extra efforts for granted: "It's just part of the service we render."

When I asked Dr. Berman to describe the worst part of his job, I was hardly prepared for his answer: "The worst part is that animals will not outlive their people."

Sobered by his response, I offered a paw in farewell. Returning to my *Vanity Fur* office, I reflected gratefully that this assignment had changed my life. Never again would I woof woefully at the sight of a friendly vet. □

"Buying lingerie for a feline has its rewards. I once bought a cat pajamas. It was interesting. I stalked into the store. Looked around. It was a little unusual. I felt like a fish out of water. Finding her size? That was easy. She's not a fat cat. Matching her purrsonality? That was a little more difficult. I had to paws to reflect on the choices. But I never had more fun."

Maidenfur offers felines over 100 ways to express their purrsonalities. Obviously, tomcats are listening.

M A I D E N F U R

Morris. Cardmember since 1980.

Finickiness
has its privileges.

Don't leave home...
order __in__ all your meals!

Slaves to Fashion

Designer dogs and couture cats show off their pet designers to MARINA SCHNAUZER

ERNIE and Norma Kama

S ome lucky animals have the good fortune to live with prominent people who dote upon their every need, every desire. While most of us undoubtedly get a fair share of love and attention, we still live rather mundane lives. Sure, we're well fed, well clothed and may even have plenty of toys to play with. But how many of us can boast of a line of clothing named after us? How many have been immortalized in the pages of high-gloss magazines? How many attend the opera, or have a regular table at Mortimer's for lunch? Among the precious few who can answer yes are the precious pets who share their lives with famous fashion designers. *V.F.* style director Marina Schnauzer visits these models of fashion, and their pet designers, at home.

ERNIE,
Norma Kamali

Ernie is a fourteen-year-old dachs-hund who still acts like a puppy. He shares his home with Norma Kamali, and until recently he ac-companied her to work daily. Ex-tremely playful, he has a whole repertoire of tricks that keep her entranced. He can lie down, roll over, speak and shake hands with either paw. Ernie has had three back operations, and when his bag of tricks fails to get him noticed, he drags his back legs to evoke sympa-thy. But Kamali is wise to his wiles. To test whether he's truly in pain, she asks him if he wants a cookie. If he leaps up and runs to the kitchen, she has her answer!

SHAWN & CAROLINE
Arnold Scaasi

Shawn and Caroline are Irish ter-riers, aged seven and three, who share a dramatic duplex apartment with Arnold Scaasi. They enjoy a spectacular view of Central Park from their huge windows. When in the city, they sleep on a pair of Biedermeier chairs; on weekends, they sleep on a pair of wing chairs.

"Fate brought us to our country house," says Scaasi. Searching for a weekend home, they finally came upon one that seemed right. While touring the rooms, he spotted a framed sepia sketch of an Irish ter-rier hanging over the fireplace.

"I thought it was an omen," he recalls, smiling.

TIM SCHAEFFER

KATE AND BRUTUS
Bill Blass

Kate and Brutus are nine-year-old golden retriever siblings. He was the giant of the litter, and she was the runt. They share a country home in Connecticut with Bill Blass, all sleeping in the same bedroom. Their first act on awakening at dawn is to go for a long walk. Weekends are devoted to discovering new territories, and the three often take half a dozen walks a day. Blass says that when he's in the country, his life is his dogs. The dogs heartily agree; on the weekends, their life is Bill.

POOKIE
Carolyne Roehm

Pookie, a West Highland white terrier, shares his opulent Park Avenue home with Carolyne Roehm. She calls him her "kindred spirit and alter ego " and says that the two favorite men in her life are her husband and Pookie. She and Pookie agree on most things, except for opera, which she adores and Pookie abhors. When Roehm first surprised her husband with Pookie, it was on an evening when they were off to the opera. She hid the tiny puppy in the folds of her opera cape and brought him along. From that evening on, whenever Pookie hears opera, he rubs his ears on the floor!

OLIVER,
TOBIAS & RUPERT
Valentino

he three dogs share with Valentino an opulent home in Rome, here they play in a magnificent arden. Oliver is American; the her two dogs, Tobias and Rupert, e English. This may account for liver's bolder personality and his ck of reserve.

Oliver is the oldest of the three gs and, as such, is afforded rtain privileges. He spends ore time traveling with Valentino d has had the designer's younger ecutive classic line named ter him.

MARIE LAURE DE DECKER

CHANEL AND LUCY
Cathy Hardwick

Chanel, three and a half, and Lucy, two and a half, are toy poodles. Chanel is champagne-colored, Lucy is a redhead (that's why she's called Lucy!). They share a luxurious apartment with Hardwick and travel upstate with her on weekends to their country home and farm. They spend their days outdoors happily chasing chickens and ducks. Poultry is their favorite food, and they are wildly excited whenever they smell a chicken or turkey in the oven. In the city, they practice their hunting skills by chasing dogs on Manhattan streets and horses in Central Park.

MAX
Michael Kors

[Ma]x was originally called Doug,
[wh]ich Michael felt was a basic no-
[non]sense name. But, says Kors,
[the] cat began to be very food-ori-
[ent]ed, and he began to feel more
[and] more like a Jewish mother,
[ply]ing his pet with tasty morsels
[and] acting generally overprotec-
[tive]. So Kors changed the cat's
[nam]e to Max, an equally basic
[na]me, only more Jewish.

[M]ax is a Devon Rex cat, a rare
[bre]ed that doesn't shed. This was
[imp]ortant to Kors, who wears a lot
[of b]lack. Max is black, white and
[gre]y, the perfect complement to
[Kor]s's minimalist fashion-color
[pal]ette, and to the stark, spare
[apa]rtment the two inhabit. Or
[may]be the inspiration worked the
[oth]er way around....

MOUJIK
Yves Saint Laurent

Moujik, a handsome French bull-dog, is Yves Saint Laurent's constant companion. Saint Laurent considers himself a "dog person," which to him means Moujik is with him always, day and night. The dog greatly enjoyed his recent trip to the U.S.S.R. when Saint Laurent was invited by Raisa Gorbachev to show his designs to the Soviet people.

Moujik has even modeled in Saint Laurent's fashion shows, once accompanying a model who was dressed in black and white to match him. His favorite fabric is taffeta; the rustling sound it makes sends him into an ecstatic frenzy.

MAXIMILLIAN
SIR LANCELOT
Geoffrey Beene

Maximillian, three and a half years old, and Sir Lancelot, three, share their Long Island country home with Geoffrey Beene. The dogs' neighbors are another pair of dachshunds who live in the house next door with *their* companion, the well-known photographer Horst. Perhaps it is Horst's friendship that has instilled an interest in photography in both Maximillian and Sir Lancelot. They keep an album of photographs of themselves, which have appeared in such periodicals as *New York*, *The New York Times Magazine*, *GQ* and *Life*. In each of the articles, they generously share the limelight with Mr. Beene.

ALFONSO
Carolina Herrera

lfonso is a four-year-old toy poo- _e who shares his New York home_ _th Sebastian, a Blue Point Hima-_ _yan, and Carolina Herrera._ _bastian is a homebody, but Al-_ _nso, seen here at the office, en-_ _ys an occasional foray into the_ _gh-fashion fast lane. He es-_ _cially loves the working day,_ _en he can reserve a coveted table_ _Mortimer's and meet Pookie, his_ _ngtime sweetheart, for lunch._ _e very mention of her name, or_ _sight of the cozy table for two at_ _ortimer's, is enough to make Al-_ _nso jump up on two feet and bark_ _th delight._ □

TAKING A
CAVALIER
ATTITUDE

SPANIEL SAVVY
Annabel, *left,* wearing
Donna Cairn, admires
a bronze sculpture
in her garden. After a
long day of being
pampered, *right,* she
relaxes in her pool
with a cool drink . . .
another typical day in
the life of a Cavalier
King Charles Spaniel.

The Cavalier King Charles Spaniel sets high standards for its people. MALTESE SCHNAYERSON asks: Would your humans make the grade?

Washington, D.C., 1988. Ronald and Nancy Reagan emerge from the helicopter behind a boisterous bundle of spaniel savvy. Flashing a winning smile and a swishing tail, First Dog Rex leads the First Family across the White House lawn, pausing briefly to turn his shiny brown eyes with practiced aplomb toward the waiting photographers. Another photo opportunity, another typical day in the charmed life of a Cavalier King Charles spaniel.

A few hundred miles away in New York City, Fred and Lowey Buckley awaken in their Park Avenue maisonette. Litter siblings of Rex Reagan, the Buckley Cavaliers share home and hearth with their socially prominent companions, Pat and William F. Buckley, Jr., in Manhattan and at their Connecticut estate. Fred and Lowey are as media savvy as their brother Rex, and are often photographed and featured in leading periodicals. They travel throughout the world with their high-profile friends, enjoying a life-style reserved for a privileged few—truly lucky dogs.

Most other dogs, like you or me, remain content with our more humble surroundings, ordinary chew toys, store-bought food and familiar spot near the foot of the bed. We can only watch and wonder what it would be like to live the elite existence of the Cavaliers. What makes them so special, so sophisticated? And why do they seem to have a knack for selecting the most indulgent human companions?

Ask any Cavalier how it feels to be pampered by the rich and famous, and he'll probably bark contentedly that he can't imagine it any other way. These small canines, unlike the rest of us, have long been accustomed to preferential treatment. Their aristocratic origins suggest that they may well be our "old biscuit" set. While the breed appears to be new in America, Cavaliers have been popular in Europe for hundreds of years. They were companions to royalty; the earliest mention of the breed occurred in 1570 by a

physician to Queen Elizabeth I. In 1587, a similar spaniel was present at the execution of her mistress, Mary, Queen of Scots. The breed's royal connection continued into the reign of King Charles II, and it was his devoted love for these special dogs that provided them with the name they bear today—the Cavalier King Charles spaniel. Legend has it that the monarch issued a royal edict that no King Charles spaniel could be denied entry to any public place and that this breed alone could run loose in London's royal parks. Little wonder, therefore, that their descendants should expect, and receive, royal treatment even today.

Americans, indeed, have embraced the Cavalier with the affection they reserve

Annabel, a gracious hostess, uses her Wedgwood tea service when entertaining her topiary friends.

for all things Anglo. Prominent people have welcomed the dogs to our shores, and their homes, by the kennel-load (and make sure it's a Louis Vuitton kennel, please).

Cavaliers have been linked to such entertainment giants as Frank Sinatra, Amy Irving and Steven Spielberg, Mia Farrow and Woody Allen, Katharine Hepburn, Liza Minnelli, Barbra Streisand, Robert Wagner, Kirk Douglas and Lauren Bacall, among others. Major Wall Street figures

like Louis Rukeyser and American Express Chairman James D. Robinson are equally enamored of the breed. Best-selling author Judith Green took up the cause of these winning little dogs. And we've already heard of their political clout in high places.... In fact, within two years of Rex's arrival at the White House in December 1985, Cavalier registrations in the United States rose by 35 percent.

Cavaliers, basking happily in the adulation of their many admirers, have a secret which we've sniffed out, one which keeps them at the top of canine society. Most purebred dogs are registered with the American Kennel Club (A.K.C.), which provides rules for the breeding, registration and showing of most breeds. Membership in the organization is selective, and those admitted feel the same pride as if they had joined an exclusive social club. Cavalier people, however, regularly hold elections in which they vote *against* affiliation with the A.K.C. They prefer their own exclusive club, the Cavalier King Charles Spaniel Club, and their own set of rules, which bar other breeds from joining. The rules are exacting and include a strict code of ethics beginning with the statement, "I feel that the welfare of the breed in general and my Cavalier[s] in particular comes before any other consideration to do with my interest in Cavaliers."

The organization forbids its members to sell Cavalier puppies to pet shops or other commercial establishments. Anyone breaking this or any of the group's nine other rules is subject to suspension or expulsion. The club maintains a puppy referral service, and there are long waiting lists for future litters. Every potential Cavalier home is screened to assess suitability. Club members are strongly encouraged to question potential Cavalier companions rigorously about the quality of life they will provide for the dogs. The responses are carefully evaluated before a Cavalier is released to a new family's care. Even President and Mrs. Reagan had to undergo stringent questioning. The nature of the questions is kept confidential, but the examination of potential homes is clearly effective.

When we consider these classy canines, we can only sigh and wonder, along with many of our readers, whether *our* people would undergo a similar examination or take and pass such an oath of allegiance!

Annabel, *large photo*, in her opulently appointed library, wearing Bow Blass. Brittany, Chloe and Amanda, *small photo far left*, are Annabel's puppies. They wear Ruff Lauren polo shirts. Elizabeth and Melissa, *center left*, share their home with Barbara and Frank Sinatra. Al, *center right*, who lives with interior designer Ann Downey, has the bold habit of carrying her own leash. Pumpkin, *above*, companion to author Judith Green, offers interior designer Mario Buatta a canapé at her Christmas party.

Dress for Excess

Kitty Glitter and Doggie Dazzlers. Faux bijoux for the four-legged set. BIRMAN BRANTLEY takes a shine to these rock stars

Go for baroque and sparkle plenty—these are the fashion buzzwords for the animal who has *everything*....Fill your vault with a dazzling collection of beautiful baubles to wear with *anything*...from denim to lamé, sweat shirt to satin, day to night. Don't bury these treasures for a rainy day...wear them now and always. They're fabulous fakes, so trot them out and strut your stuff. You're sure to turn a few heads, but hey, isn't that what you intended in the first place?

1. Diamante "milk-bones" make a delicious addition to your sweat shirt. Imported crystals set in gold or silver, by Wendy Gell.

2. Mickey and Minnie Mouse on the rocks? Yes, and they've never looked better! Your favorite rodents are now brooches in crystal and pearl combinations, by Wendy Gell.

3. Great Scott! It's Scotties and poodles in sparkly pavé. These brooches are avail-able in both black and white crystal. Some designs are accented by silver cha leashes and doghouse or bone motifs. dog's life has never looked better! Jewe designed by Monty Don.

4. Wildcats, show your spots (or stripe by collecting a group of "panther" pin Inspired by the gems made famous by th Duchess of Windsor, these brooches a enameled with the vivid patterns of jung cats. The jet crystal collar is clasped wi a rhinestone snow-tiger face. Collar ar pins designed by Kenneth J. Lane.

5. Terriers are the well-bred choice f daytime jewels. Golden or silvery terrie have heads that move. The pair of stridir Scotties is enameled black for great authenticity. Jewelry designed by Butl and Wilson.

6. A crystal panther clutches a gold rir in his mouth to form the centerpiece of dramatic collar. The cluster of gold chains forms the ties that bind you to th exotic design by Butler and Wilson. ☐

JIM BUCK'S SCHOOL FOR DOGS
He feels that acceptance in the program, as at any
fine school, is a privilege that must be earned.

Take a Walk on the Wild Side

Pampered pooches meet their match in Jim Buck, the ultimate dog-walker. DOBERMAN DUNNE joins the leader of the pack on his morning rounds

BRUCE PLOTKIN

Jim Buck, the quintessential dog-walker, "taking care of the family dog in New York."

W'e're not in the cute-dog business. We're more like Camp Lejeune." These were the first words spoken to me by Jim Buck, the quintessential dog-walker. Or perhaps I should say "barked" at me, for his gruff tone matched my own. It's the voice he must use to elicit respect from the four-legged set. I think of myself as a pretty tough character—most Dobermans are. Yet his tone got to me. It let me know who had the upper hand. I sat down at respectful attention and listened to his story.

This former navy man takes his profession—"taking care of the family dog in New York: training, breeding, showing, handling"—very seriously. He has been in the business for more than thirty years and may have invented the idea of professional dog-walking. He came upon the concept quite by accident. One day, while walking his Great Dane, Nimble, in Central Park, he noticed an Airedale attacking a German shepherd. Reacting quickly, he flung a rock at the Airedale, knocking him cold. The dog's owner rushed up and, to Buck's astonishment (as well as my own!), thanked him warmly for interceding. She then asked him to work with her dog, Benjamin, to civilize him and "teach him some manners." The request struck a responsive chord in Buck. Using a fox-hunting horn and whip (relics of his upbringing), he managed to instill a sense of discipline in the overindulged animal. His success with Benjamin spread quickly by word of mouth on Manhattan's Upper East Side, and before long Buck was training a regular group of canine ruffians in Central Park after work each evening.

One day, after viewing his career prospects in the family shipping business and finding himself emotionally unfulfilled, he broke with tradition and quit to devote himself to the dog-training business full-time.

"Now there's a man after my own heart," I thought, but his family's reaction was far less enthusiastic. Buck was married and the father of three children. A self-described "Park Avenue brat," he had attended prestigious schools and was a member of the well-known Buck family, for which Bucks County in Pennsylvania is named. He was

---

…dogs had always been an avocation in the family, never a vocation. The family hoped that Jim was just going through a phase, but the phase has now lasted more than thirty years.

---

the product of a marriage of two great steel fortunes—on his mother's side, U.S. Steel, on his father's, Bethlehem Steel. At the time, the family's interests included steamships and investment banking. Dog-training would hardly do. One uncle, James A. Farrell, was an American Kennel Club judge at the Westminster Kennel Club show, and the family did raise and show fox terriers and greyhounds. But dogs had al-

ways been an avocation in the family, nev a vocation. The family hoped that Jim w just going through a phase, but the phas has now lasted more than thirty years. A Jim Buck is happy—physically fit, em tionally renewed and fiscally sound. Thir years of dog-walking have put his thr sons through college. One of them is Paine Webber; another is a chemical an lyst; a third son runs a wildlife preserve upstate New York. In addition to all this, is a weekend country squire who show horses in Connecticut. I listened avidly his every word. His voice held me e tranced. I realized that, even though we h just met, I was eager to gain his respe And I wanted to hear more about his profe sional devotion to my fellow canines.

The business, he went on to tell me, h evolved slowly from humble beginnings its present size. Jim Buck's School f Dogs now services nine packs of dogs ea day. Each group is supervised by two do walkers, and Buck is quick to point out th of all the dog-walking services in Ne York, his is the only one with two train handlers assigned to every pack of dog The pack can vary in size from four dogs over twenty, depending on the temper ment of the pack's members and the expe ence of the dog-handlers. The handlers a selected with great care. After extensi training and an apprenticeship period, th are entrusted with their own group of do but still share ultimate reponsibility wi their co-handlers. This system ensures th no dogs are ever left unattended.

The service is in effect from Mond through Friday. The first dogs are picked at 6:30 A.M.; the last ones are return home at 11:00 A.M. Afternoons are reserv for interviews with prospective clien and for intensive training sessions for so of the "problem children" or new gro members.

The phone rings: a prospective client.

terview is arranged. The client thinks the main purpose of the meeting is to become informed about Buck and his service. But for Buck, even more important is checking out the compatibility of the people and their dogs to determine how well the animal is likely to get along with others in the group. He feels that acceptance in the program, as any fine school, is a privilege that must be earned. During a typical interview, he looks the dog in the eye. After more than thirty years, he is convinced he can tell a great deal about the dog's personality from how his gaze is returned. I make a special effort to look confident and in control as he continues. He sometimes examines the bloodlines of a purebred dog to determine characteristic personality traits. He meets the dog's family. Are they nice? Does the dog seem happy and well-suited to his people? Are there children? How do they behave? I bark that his approach bears a certain resemblance to *grrroup therapy*," but he feels that there is much to be learned about the dog from the children in the family. If they are well-behaved and well-adjusted, it is likely that the animal will too.

Sometimes people choose a dog that is more than they can handle. Buck feels it makes little sense for him to spend his time training a renegade. "A lot of people buy a bear' and feel if they love it enough, it will become a cuddly dog. But it will still be a bear.'" Buck pays particular attention to the mothers and children because they are the ones who spend the most time actually taking care of the dogs. If he can educate them well, his job is made much easier. He also examines the fathers, who sometimes unwittingly make his job a difficult one. They can undo all his training by indulging and spoiling their four-legged companions. 'Dogs need interaction," said Buck. "It's different than kids playing in the park. Our group is not unlike a playgroup. It's the same program that kids get at home. We're not walking dogs for lazy people. We instill good manners, fitness, and create a knowledgeable and skilled owner. We believe in pride of ownership."

"A dog doesn't have to be big to need a workout," he continued. "Terriers need to work out their aggression. Big dogs need to work out, too, because they can get lazy and degenerate. City dogs are far superior to country dogs. Suburban dogs are lazy— they're often ignored in the backyard. Country dogs roam, get hit by cars, poi-

soned, shot by people hunting deer. City dogs have to be scheduled for activity. Most other dogs don't get this degree of attention and concern."

The dog-walking business is volatile, according to Buck. Summers are slower than the other seasons. Nevertheless, the service continues through the slow months because dogs who have gone away are frequently indulged by their owners. They often need a bit of reinforcement to regain discipline on their return to city life and their group.

Among Buck's clients are many prominent New Yorkers: lawyers, physicians, Wall Street executives, media and political figures. But they remain anonymous; Buck is communicative about the dogs but discreet about their owners.

Dog-walking can be viewed as a social and economic barometer. "This is a tough business, very competitive. And our service is the first thing cut from the budget when things go bad. Some clients have been quietly kept on the rolls during difficult financial periods. In fact," Buck smiles, "a very famous stock analyst calls me at home to ask about my business, as an economic indicator."

The dogs sometimes inadvertently reveal family secrets. "You can't own a dog in an unstable, unstructured environment," says Buck. When a formerly well-groomed dog suddenly appears unkempt, it can mean a rift or problem in the family. Drug users tend to abuse or neglect their dogs. The

animals may be underfed. Some dogs have led the pack into a bar or an unfamiliar apartment house, which may mean that the animal's owner frequently stops off for a drink or an assignation with a girlfriend. (It's amazing how much we dogs can reveal, even though we cannot speak....)

I accompanied Buck early one morning on his rounds. He awakens at 5:00 A.M. each weekday and meets with his handlers at 6:00. We picked up the first dog at 6:30. Within an hour, after numerous stops along Park and Fifth avenues and on the lovely tree-lined streets of the Upper East Side, our pack of twenty-four dogs was complete. We bounded down Fifth Avenue to Central Park, where we walked at a brisk pace, passing joggers and New Yorkers on their way to work. Over several little bridges we went, through tunnels, a quick spin around the museum (with ample "rest stops"—Buck thoughtfully carries a supply of newspaper in his back pocket). I was left feeling rather breathless. The regular canine group took this brisk workout in stride—for them, it was all in a day's work.

By 11:00 A.M., nearly all the dogs in the group had been returned to their homes. Heading down Park Avenue with the last few pack members, we were stopped by a woman who complained, "You shouldn't be walking those dogs down Park Avenue." "Madame, these dogs *live* on Park Avenue," Buck replied with a smile, and continued on his way without missing a step. □

"GRRROUP THERAPY": Training a regular group of canine ruffians in Central Park.

PHOTOS BY BRUCE PLOTKIN

Sweater Girls (and Boys)

Dogs want—deserve—to dress as well as their human companions. Until recently, we found this difficult to achieve in the U.S. The true fashion hounds among us had to indulge their passion for fashion with the transatlantic creations of Yves Saint Bernard, Karl Dogerfeld, Emanuel Ungrrro, Catfish Dior and other top-dog European designers. If we yearned for something chic or outré, we had to follow the scent to the elegant pet emporiums of London or Paris. But America has finally caught up with her foreign cousins, and top U.S. fashion designers are offering exciting new wares for the furry domestic market.

Designers like Canine Klein, Ruff Lauren, Geoffrey Bone and Cavalier Roehm join forces with Liz Clawborne and Adrienne Vittadogi to produce designs that are setting canine couture on its ear. We mutts-à-la-mode have always had the desire to show our true colors—now we have a way to wear them proudly. From bold geometric patterns, like the Scottie-check design worn by Nubie (bottom row, left) to the soft femininity of the garland-of-roses sweater worn by Annabel (top row, left), the designs reflect a new sense of taste and style certain to be appreciated by any canine eager to express his or her individuality. The innovative collection features dozens of styles; surely one or more will catch your fancy. It even introduces an exclusive group of "Mother-Doggie Fashions," so your human companions (grown-ups or kids) can dress to reflect your unique sense of style.

Fashionable felines should not be put off by the fact that dogs wear these fashions. Sweaters in small or medium sizes should be a purrfect fit...and the tiger stripe is sure to be a favorite with any wildcat in your furry circle!
—**ROBERT GREYHOUND**

Photographed by BRUCE PLOTKIN

Lick Your Chops bakes fabulous fresh cookies for us dapper dogs
(and cool cats, too) daily. But the cookie doesn't crumble there.
RON RUSSIAN BLUE follows the scent to the newest animal emporium

Doggie's Cookies

Pet customers, *opposite p*
sniff out their favorite coo
from the vast selection. F
for thought, *left*, and for
consumption as well.

hocolate, apple cinnamon, peanut butter, liver chip…*Liver chip?* While we admit that this may be an acquired aste, the liver chip cookies are a big faorite at the popular New York watering ole for the furry set. Lick Your Chops akes fresh cookies for cats and dogs like s daily in a staggering array of shapes nd flavors, including the more savory arieties like cheese quackers, rye bones, hicken, beef, ham, veggie, carrot, and ven liver fire hydrants. The shop is nown for its fresh-baked biscuits, availble individually or in delightful gift packages, and also carries a complete selection of foods, supplies, gifts and books for us and our human companions.

Lick Your Chops calls itself a complete department store for animal people. While this may be true in a sense (because—fair is fair—the folks we live with do foot the bill), we animals prefer to think of it as our own pet emporium. Where else can we find the latest in nutritionally sound foods, beds, carriers, toys and more. Indeed, anything needed to make our lives comfortable, healthy and enjoyable is likely to be found here.

From its humble beginnings as a small store in a suburb of New York City, Lick Your Chops has expanded to include six stores, with more being planned. Indeed, not long ago an outpost of the company was set up in Bloomingdog's (Oops! I meant Bloomingdale's) fashionable Lexington Avenue store.

Lick Your Chops prides itself on its comprehensive selection of merchandise. But if you ask any of us satisfied fourlegged patrons why we shop there, it's dollars to dog biscuits we'll bark unanimously: It's for the cookies! ☐

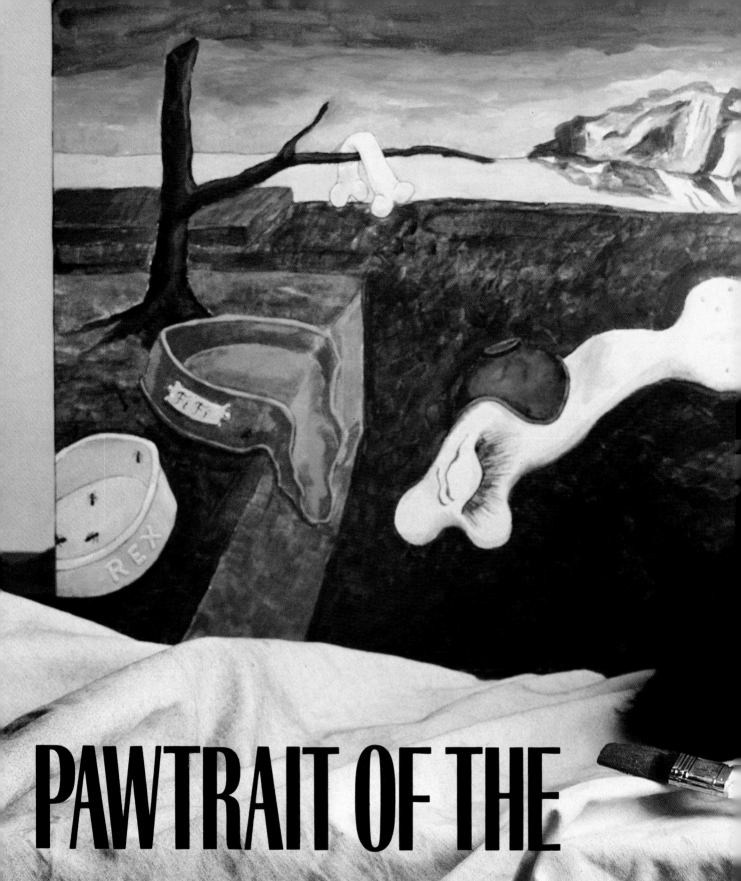

PAWTRAIT OF THE ARTIST AS A YOUNG DOG

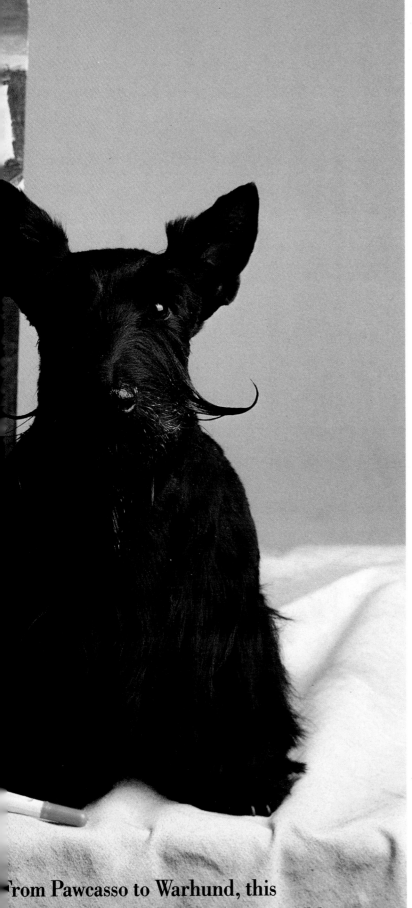

Canines have always had one paw in the art world. From the earliest cave drawings to the contemporary works found in galleries today, our four-legged ancestors have played an important role in the development of art. Most of us, however, are barking mad at the treatment of dogs in the annals of art history. While we often appear as the *subject* of a work of art, our contribution as the *artist* has largely been ignored. The canine creators of arf art have gone largely unrecognized outside of dogdom.

To correct this situation, *Vanity Fur* presents a pack of dog artists who are well known for their unique vision and innovative techniques only in the canine art world. These gifted artists share that special quality found in all creative creatures, an all-consuming passion for their work. You might say they are dogged by their art.

SALVADOR DOGI's eccentric character was reflected in his own manner of dress and grooming, as well as in his art. A leading proponent of the Dogdog school of art, he painted surrealistic dreamscapes populated by unusual, seemingly unrelated, elements. *The Persistence of Mealtime*, shown here, combined his familiar imagery of melting dog dishes, signifying the passage of mealtimes, with a human face that was transforming into a bone. This seemed to suggest the human being assuming the role of canine caretaker.

Paintings by TERRY JOHNSON

Photographed by BRUCE PLOTKIN

From Pawcasso to Warhund, this pack of pup painters sets the art world barking. Six who are dogged by their art. BOB COLLIECELLO reports

◄ Salvador Dogi

...everyone would be famous for fifteen minutes

ANDY WARHUND was the poppa of Pup Art. His statement that everyone would be famous for fifteen minutes has unhappily been true of his own artistic reputation in the world of two-legged collectors. He painted commercial art icons like the Alpo can shown here, but many did not find his art in good taste. Most dogs preferred the flavor of the food being illustrated. His unfortunate and unexpected demise brought renewed attention to his work. We have lost a great talent, but his special vision will surely influence a new generation of canine artists.

PABLO PAWCASSO was the master of many styles of art. From the circus dogs of his harlequin paintings to the geometric forms in his cubist canines, he conveyed the total image in an economy of lines. The simplicity of his brushstrokes belied the complexity of his message. He was always one, or *four*, pawsteps ahead of his peers. Pawcasso will be remembered as one of the great forces of the muttern art movement.

◄ Andy Warhund
Pablo Pawcasso ►

...broken
og dishes, as a new
art medium

INCENT VAN DOGH embodied a rare
rm of genius. In spite of his intense and
latile personality, which kept him in
d out of obedience schools in an unsuc-
ssful attempt to bring some order into
s life, Van Dogh found the time to paint
untingly beautiful pawtraits, land-
apes, and still-lifes like the one shown
re. His contemporaries thought he was
ne sick puppy," and he never sold a
inting during his lifetime. Despondent,
bit off his own ear (which was quite an
complishment in its own right). Iron-
lly, however, his work now fetches
gh prices at auction. His painting of a
se of dogwood blossoms, for example,
s recently sold for 50,000,000 bones to
apanese Chin.

JULIAN SCHNAUZER is an artist on
e cutting edge of the art world. One of
e "new image" artists, he is exploring
e introduction of everyday elements,
e broken dog dishes, as a new art me-
um. Never before has the statement
he medium is the message" been as true
it is here.

◄ Vincent Van Dogh
Julian Schnauzer ►

The movers and shakers in the dog world identified with this bold new movement and coined it "abstract destructivism."

JACKSON PAWLOCK was best known for his innovative "drip" technique. His first painting was inadvertently created when he returned home from a walk in the rain and shook off his muddy coat on a white carpet. Art critics were taken with the power of his work and its monumental scale, which they attributed to the vigorous action of the whole body. Well-heeled art collectors, the movers and shakers in the dog world, identified with this bold new movement and coined it "abstract destructivism." White carpets have never been the same! □

◄ Jackson Pawlock

MORRIS:

A Cat for Our Times

st when it seemed the world had gone to the dogs, we were offered the chance

r a new breed of leadership. Morris the Cat was a Presidential possibility

ho would make a difference — a candidate who could see (even in the dark!)

e solutions to our pressing national problems. When he entered the race in

gust 1987, the country seemed ready for a four-legged leader. But Morris

ocked Americans with his sudden withdrawal just months before the election.

AIL SHEDDY examines Morris's unprecedented campaign

With an innovative set of public pawlicies, he jumped into the race boldly with all four paws....

What great things would the country have achieved with a cat at the helm? Would the candidate's pawlicies have changed the direction of American politics?

These questions swirled in the minds of Morris's disappointed supporters as they padded out of the news conference. They had entered the room with giddy optimism, only to be shattered by the news that their great leader would withdraw from political life. Morris urged them not to lament his decision. His campaign, in his estimation, had been a success. Great strides had been made for felines. It had been a monumental year for cats. But now he felt he needed to devote his full energies to the cat food business.

Morris had won the support of the feline population of the country, buoying their spirits with crowd-pleasing slogans like "Walk softly and carry a big can opener," and "Din-din in every dish and a litter box on every corner." He had developed an innovative set of public pawlicies, including beliefs on animal rights: "Fur coats should be limited to those who can grow them," and drugs: "Say 'no' to catnip." His message was strong and the public was behind him, despite the fact that he, like Geraldine Ferraro and Jessie Jackson, was purrceived as a member of a minority group. He knew that the challenges facing a feline candidate would be great, but he jumped boldly into the race with all four paws. Like Ronald Reagan, Clint Eastwood, and Sonny Bono, he was a screen star leaping from Hollywood onto the politcal stage. He was determined to be taken seriously by the American voter.

When Morris first entered the race, it was fraught with controversy. Gary Hart's impropriety prompted Morris to remark, "You won't catch me catting around," and "The media is welcome to follow my tail." True to his word, the bachelor candidate had only the most chaste dinners with female feline friends. The Iran-Contra scandal elicited the comments, "I may shed, but I don't shred," and "Any cat would have smelled a rat." He promised to purrsonally give a good licking to anyone on his staff caught getting his paws dirty.

Reflecting the philosophy of his fellow felines, Morris chose to run as an independent. This stance allowed him to continue his longtime practice of ignoring people regardless of their party affiliation. Morris gained tremendous support for this position. In fact, a political poll conducted by the Opinion Research Corporation found Morris ranked high among the Presidential hopefuls. He was recognized by more than

> ' You won't catch me catting around, and the media is welcome to follow my tail. '

70% of the respondents, a significant lead over Robert Dole (67%), Jack Kemp (59%), Richard Gephardt (53%), Paul Laxalt (40%) and Bruce Babbitt (33%). Indeed, these candidates dropped out of the race before he did. Remarkable Michael Dukakis, who was recognized by only 41% of the respondents, quickly gained in popularity and recognition, owing in part to the prominence of his cousin, Olympia Dukakis, who won an Academy Award (indication that a Hollywood connection can sometimes be a plus).

The campaign took Morris all over the country—from Philadelphia for the Bicentennial Celebration of the Constitution, to New York City, San Diego, Tampa, Houston, Boston. In every city, people flocked to see his pawtitions. He could almost feel the softness of that big chair in the Oval Office.

When June rolled around, Morris got a leap on the competition by being the first candidate to announce his running mate. Adhering to the doctrine that "all cats are created equal, regardless of gender, color or breed," he selected Keller, a black-and-orange-striped mixed-breed spay from Iowa, to run on his ticket.

But a few weeks later, Morris took a break from heavy campaigning and spent a quiet evening at home. It was this night that changed history. Morris thought, and thought, and paced the floor. Becoming President had seemed like the greatest calling in the world. But then he realized: If he sat in the President's chair at the White House, he'd be busy attending to *human* causes—meeting with world leaders, the Cabinet, the Official Astrologer. Morris knew he had a responsibility to cats...his true constituency. Sacrificing his ambition was no small thing, but he would do so for the welfare of his fellow felines.

Before descending from the stage, Morris scanned the hushed crowd, let his eyes pause briefly to meet the gaze of individual members of his loyal constituency, and raised one eloquent paw in solidarity with the crowd. In one great year he had stalked the political trail, carrying high the banner for felines. America's cats sought opportunity, and Morris made their dreams a reality. Now, with a new vision, he will make good on his campaign promise, ensuring that there is a satisfied cat in every kitchen across America.□

PRETENTIOUS PETS

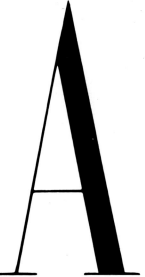

American animals have taken a lion's share of ribbing from our British cousins about our pampered life-styles. We American pets are famous—or notorious—all over the world for our luxurious homes, wardrobes and diets. The international media are quick to point a finger at our indulgences, hardly letting us enjoy our goodies in peace.

Word has recently reached our shores of a remarkable social movement begun in England by a lone Cavalier King Charles spaniel named China. She has inspired her human companion, one Francesca Findlater, to create all manner of delightful, entertaining and really useful products for the enlightened furry masses. Ms. Findlater has written a book called *The Sloane Rover's Handbook*. Researched by China, it is an indispensable guide to the Sloane life-style for the "in" pooch. ("Sloane Rover" is the British functional equivalent to our "Yuppie Puppy.")

The handbook is the very last bark in the Sloane Rover attitude, including choice of name (Happy, Dookie, Spot and Phideaux are recommended), neighborhood, diet, wardrobe, education and exercise. Strict adherence to the entire program is essential to the creation of an impeccable image.

After establishing themselves as the ultimate arbiters of Sloane petdom, China and Ms. Findlater set up a mail-order service called Pretentious Pets. The company offers a charming assortment of products necessary to maintain the appropriate level of indulgence (and humor) in our pampered life-style. The more original items include "The Pretentious Pets Anti-Smog Air Purifier/Nuclear Defense Suit (PPASAP for short). Already tried and tested, this ultimate little outfit will protect you from the perils of either impending nuclear holocaust (long-term) or (short-term) the traumas of exhaust fumes and roads littered with unscooped poop."

Other popular items are "the present of the eighties…The Ultimate Pretentious Pets Doggi-Dom." Yes, at last the answer to the nagging question, "What happens if 'love' strikes and your person has left his condom at home?" Well, in true, dependable Saint Bernard fashion, you can come to the rescue. The jolly johnny comes in an attractive package that attaches discreetly to your collar. "When the moment strikes…you just come when you're called!" Or, "alternatively, for those people with taste, discrimination and money to spend on indulging you, the Pretentious Pets Personalized Share Portfolio is at hand. A personalized stock portfolio is the ideal gift. Consult with our leading stockbrokers and let them select a perfect package of stocks and bonds for you with a minimum investment of £100." Yet another item: "Pet Predictions…a team of astrologers will specially prepare your birth chart."

Less outrageous choices are a toy mink mouse or chew bone, packed with a small bottle of champagne (ostensibly for the people, but we know who really deserves it!); the Christmas collar replete with holly and ornaments; or the delightfully understated gold-plated Pretentious Pets bone-shaped dog tags, which can be engraved on the reverse side with your name and address.

Who says the British don't have a sense of humor? (Though we do wonder why it took them so long to catch up to the rest of us….) □

…an indispensable guide to the Sloane life-style for the "in" pooch.

PARTY

Are you into cross-dressing?
No, we're not referring to anything
with sinister undertones, or
going on a gender-bender. We're
talking about pulling a species switch.
Have you ever wondered how the
other half lives? Try dressing up as
a pig, a bunny, or a reindeer.
See what it's like to take a walk on the
wild side (undomesticated, that is).

Simplicity Pattern Company
home-sewing pattern for animal costumes,
number 8936. Available
wherever patterns are sold.

ANIMALS

Cars

THE RANGE FOR ROVER

Designer Ruff Lauren test-drives the new Range Rover.

BY MUTT GINSBURG

Ruff Lauren rides "off-road" in the Range Rover.

Ruff Lauren. The name is synonymous with tasteful refinement and well-bred style. This top-dog designer is recognized all over the world as a creator of canine clothes that work. His typical look is a combination of carefully assembled elements that add up to a seemingly effortless elegance—a throwaway chic that looks easy, if you know how.

Ruff is the embodiment of his own philosophy. A neighborhood dog from the streets, he cultivated his bark and gait to emulate that of the pedigreed hounds on the tony dog-show circuit. He forged a new image for himself and, like the clothes, it works. This is a dog who can live in both worlds, equally at home in a pickup truck or a Porsche. Fortunately, he has the means, as well as the style, to own both. We knew that this was a dog who would appreciate the cachet and performance of a new entry in the American luxury car market. Or was it the new entry in the American utility vehicle market? We asked Ruff Lauren to test-drive the new Range Rover to find out.

"First of all, I'm struck by the name," he barked in his inimitable way. "It is *so* appropriate for a vehicle that will certainly appeal to the canine market." The car, which contains seats for five, also has a roomy rear compartment which can easily accommodate a few more. Remarking on the beautifully crafted leather seats, one of the few options available on the fully loaded, well-appointed vehicle, he added, "Leather seats make sense. They don't catch or hold shedding hair, and if there's—how shall I say?—an accident, it can be wiped clean in a breeze."

Positioning himself behind the wheel, he commented on the arrangement of the driver's seat and windows that afforded him a clear, unobstructed view of the road. "Similar to the view from my truck. But much nicer." He turned the key in the ignition and eased the stick shift for the four-speed automatic transmission into drive. "I understand that the American Range Rovers are only available with automatic transmission." Eyeing the second stick shift that controlled the variable differential of the four-wheel drive, which is always in effect, he added, "Maybe this is a good idea. It could become complicated if you found yourself shifting *both* controls at once."

The car started up without a hitch, and he pulled away from the curb and headed onto a winding country road. "The car holds the curves well," he remarked, "but there's more play in the steering wheel than in my Porsche. It feels more like the power steering on an American car than on a European model."

Reaching the highway, he accelerated to cruising speed. The car remained quiet and comfortable. The automatic cruise control was engaged, and we turned on the stereo system. The glove box contained a cassette tape about off-road driving, so he popped it in. Strains of stately music vaguely reminiscent of "Masterpiece Theatre" filled the car; we felt as if we were being filmed for a Range Rover commercial. A well-modulated voice, clearly a product of Oxford or Cambridge, intoned on the correct procedure for negotiating off-road terrain. Smiling a bit at the posh pronouncements, we pulled out the tape. At the

next exit, we pulled off the highway.

Not "off-road," mind you, but onto the smoothly paved ramp of a local shopping mall, confirming the assumption of Roger Beagle, the U.S. marketing director of Range Rover: "Our puppy polls show us that our canine customers want to know the pedigree of the vehicle and its performance record at field trials. But like most dogs, they don't necessarily want to take the car through its paces themselves."

We pulled into the first available parking space, and after a brief stop at Bloomingdog's to inspect a Ruff Lauren display, returned to the car for the short drive home.

As the vehicle was eased into reverse, the silence was shattered by a loud, grating squeak. We heard it again every time Ruff applied the brake while the car was in reverse. A Corgi rapped on the window, and Ruff lowered it to hear what the dog had to say.

"I see you have a new Range Rover, too. Or should I say, I *heard* you have one. My car also squeaks when it's in reverse. I've come to think of it as the Rover's call of the wild! I brought it in for servicing, and they told me that they'd encountered the problem before. They just don't know what's causing it. Or how to correct it. But they're working on it. In the meantime, I've gotten rather used to it. In fact, it makes a handy way to meet other like-minded dogs on the road. Happy Rovering!" he barked brightly, and ambled away.

Ruff shrugged and said, "I guess it's just the price you pay for being one of the first in America to drive the new status symbol. Maybe it's a form of reverse snobbery. An annoying little problem you share with the others who can afford thirty thousand dollars plus for a utility vehicle."

Or maybe, I thought, it was just the British having the last laugh. To coin a phrase, they could hear us coming. □

Ruff Lauren and the Range Rover— tasteful refinement and well-bred style.

Wine

THE LAP OF LUXURY

Cats' favorite light white beverage isn't tap water anymore.

BY JOEL L. FLUFFMAN

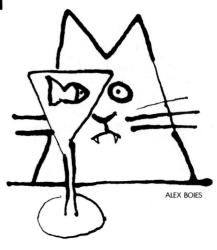

ALEX BOIES

Ask sophisticated felines about their favorite light, white beverage, and until recently they might well have said it was their local tap water. But not today, when the average cat is a far cry from the humble mouser of generations past. Today's cat, like his human companion, seeks more culinary excitement at mealtime. Typical feline dinner offerings include exotic combinations of crab and shrimp, beef, veal and even pasta, a selection hardly comparable to the catch-as-catchcan dinner of mouse available to the cat of yesteryear.

Dull, flat tap water is hardly the beverage of choice to accompany the new delectable dinner options. The modern cat is more daring in his approach to drinking. He is willing to experiment with unusual new beverages; his palate is ready for new flavor experiences.

Many cats have trained their people to indulge them with the elaborate dinners that are now de rigueur. It is only a small step to convince them to provide an appropriate beverage to accompany the tastier meals and create a new level of culinary adventure. Pampered, special cats like yourself, or other felines of your acquaintance, are entitled to pop open a bottle of the bubbly to celebrate festive occasions. The lap of luxury, if we may permit ourselves a small pun, is your due. You owe it to yourself, but more than that, your people owe it to you. Bubbly here, incidentally, does not refer to sparkling water like Purrier, though even that would be a marked improvement over tap water. It refers to Chatpagne. Purrier Jouët, for example, is an excellent choice. Save it for a special celebration, like the first time your people serve you seafood. *Real* seafood, not the canned variety. And for those really special occasions (a litter of kittens—or *no* litter of kittens), break out the Purrier Jouët rosé (we just adore its little blush and the delicate way the bubbles wet our whiskers!).

Average mealtimes, those typical Monday-through-Friday days, deserve the little lift that the appropriate beverage choice provides. There are several unpretentious wines available that will brighten your mealtime without setting your people back an exorbitant amount of money. These little extras make dining a gracious and memorable experience.

Viña San Pedro, a winery in Santiago, Chile, produces three wines that are unusually good values. Their *Gato Blanco* (White Cat, for those of you who don't speak Spanish) is a delightful Sauvignon blanc. This light, dry white wine, with its blend of Sémillon and Sauvignon grapes, is very similar to a French Graves or California Sauvignon blanc. Moderately priced, it's an ideal choice for a wine to accompany your fish or pasta meals.

Gato Negro (Black Cat) is a Cabernet Sauvignon, a light, dry red wine similar to a red Bordeaux. This reasonably priced, delicate red wine, a blend of Cabernet and Merlot grapes, is the perfect complement to a meal of veal, lamb or pork. An added bonus to the two wines just mentioned is the delightful little cat charm that hangs from the neck of every bottle, a white charm with the *Blanco*, a black one with the *Negro*. We suggest that you collect them, to create a cunning little charm necklace in a week or two. . . .

Viña San Pedro also produces a premium red wine which they call *Gato de Oro* (Gold Cat). This wine, too, is a Cabernet Sauvignon, but it is made entirely from Cabernet grapes. The resulting wine is light and dry, but with a heavier finish, similar to a red Bordeaux, a Margaux or a Pomerol. This smoother, more elegant wine is perfect to drink now with beef, veal or pasta or to lay away to enjoy in the future. We feel it's a value hard to beat.

Apéritif wines are a good choice before meals or after dinner. Some cats mix their apéritif with club soda or white wine for a drink similar to Kir. Many mixes are popular, but milk combinations are to be avoided, as the resulting drink has a nasty tendency to curdle. Dubonnet Rouge (red) or Dubonnet Blanc (white) are two especially good apéritif choices. The labels feature an illustration of a cat, so we know we're prime apéritif consumers. The white is a light, refreshing drink, the red a bit heavier. Dubonnet is a touch sweet; many prefer it as a mixed drink.

Zeller Schwarze Katz (Black Cat) is a German Moselle wine. Moselles come in three different grades: Kabinett, the driest; Auslese, the sweetest; and Spätlese, which is in between. Moselle wines are not as dry as Chablis or as sweet as Sauterne.

Zeller Schwarze Katz should not be imbibed with a meal, but rather used as an apéritif. Kabinett is the best before-meal choice and Auslese is the best after-dinner selection. Moselles can be used right away or can be held for five years from the date on the bottle; Auslese can be laid away for seven to ten years. The best years for these wines are 1983 and '85; avoid 1982, which was not up to standard. A Moselle like *Zeller Schwarze Katz* is the perfect accompaniment to a snack of cheese and fruit. Or even cheese and mice, for though gourmet dining is the way to go today, an occasional snack of mice can be a most enjoyable touch of nostalgia.

Some cats do not wish to drink the same beverage as their people do. Some cats fancy a drink that was created just for them, with their own special tastes in mind. For such fussy felines, we recommend Catnip Liqueur. This liquid ambrosia is distilled from catnip. One lap will leave you light-headed and tingly—the effect is intoxicating. Truly, the lap of luxury was never more divine. □

CREDITS

Pages 14-15 (Books): *The Dog in Art* by Robert Rosenblum, Harry N. Abrams, 100 Fifth Avenue, New York, NY 10011. Tel. (212) 206-7715.

Pages 16 and 18-19 (Art): William Wegman Polaroids represented by The Pace Macgill Gallery, 11 East 57th Street, New York, NY 10022. Tel. (212) 759-7999.

Page 22 (Living Room Leopards): The California Spangled Cat, Paul Casey, 7211 Clybourne Avenue, Sun Valley, CA 91352. Tel. (818) 503-9511. **(Bone Appétit):** Chocolate of Champions, V.I.P. Sweets, The Brewery, 30 Germania Street, Jamaica Plain, MA 02130. Tel. (617) 243-4030. **(Cat Boxes):** Site, 35 North Main Street, New Hope, PA 18938. Tel. (215) 862-2660. **(Heavy Petting):** The Argyle Fountain Spa, 294 Country Club Road, Argyle, TX 76226. Tel. (817) 464-7231.

Page 24 (Art for the Furry Masses): The Dog Museum of America, 1721 S. Mason, Saint Louis, MO 63131. Tel. (314) 821-DOGS. William Secord Fine Arts, 263A West 19th Steet, Suite 815, New York, NY 10011. Tel. (212) 929-5793. The Sara Davenport Gallery, 206 Walton Street, London SW3 2JL, England, 01-225-2223/4. Jay Johnson Inc., America's Folk Heritage Gallery, 1044 Madison Avenue, New York, NY 10021. Tel. (212) 628-7280. **(Sweet Smell of Success):** Le Chien, 1461A First Avenue, New York, NY 10021. Tel. (212) 861-8100.

Page 25 (Stamp of Approval): Inkadinkadoo, 105 South Street, Boston, MA 02111. Tel. (617) 426-3458. **(Designs for Living):** Carl D'Aquino and Geo. Wm. Humphreys, Jr., Interiors, 520 Broadway, 7th floor, New York, NY 10012. Tel. (212) 925-1770.

Page 26 (She's a Real Doll): Barbie Dog, Suzanne Codi, 111 Quincy Place N.E., Washington, DC 20002. Bone Jour Café, 2818 Pennsylvania Avenue N.W. Washington, D.C. 20007. Tel. (202) 333-8349. **(Dog Gone):** Traveling with Man's Best Friend, Dawbert Press, Inc., P.O. Box 2758, Duxbury, MA 02331. Tel. (617) 934-7202. **(Perpetual Care):** Living Free Animal Sanctuary, P.O. Box 283, Mountain Center, CA 92361. Tel. (714) 659-4686.

Page 28 (Plush Mush): Trophée Revillon, Revillon, Inc., 333 Seventh Avenue, New York, NY 10001. Tel. (212) 563-4122. **(Proxy Pets):** Video Dog and Cat, Creative Programming, 30 East 60th Street, New York, NY 10022. Tel. (212) 688-9100. **(Celebrity Pet Pri-**

orities): Center for Pet Therapy, 860 United Nations Plaza, Suite 9G, New York, NY 10017. Tel. (212) 535-3917. Bashkim Dibra, Fieldston Pets, 3476 Bailey Avenue, Riverdale, NY 10463. Tel. (212) 796-4541.

Page 29 (In the Swim): The Annual Dog Swim, Sports Department, Canadian National Exhibition, Toronto, Ontario, M6K 3C3. Canada. **(The Best Little Cat House):** Haute Feline, L. Coffey, Ltd., 4244 Linden Hills Boulevard, Minneapolis, MN 55410. Tel (612) 925-3209. **(Get a Head):** Dobermask, Creative Imaginations, P.O. Box 2649, Costa Mesa, CA 92628. Tel. (213) 945-9571.

Page 34 (Run for Your Life): Greyhound Friends, Inc., 2 Sacramento Place, Cambridge, MA 02138. Tel. (617) 354-3669. **(Best Bytes):** FYDO, Treat-Care Technologies, Inc., 17 Crescent Street, Stamford, CT 06906. Tel. (203) 964-0909. **(All in the Family):** Mario Buatta, Inc., 120 East 80th Street, New York, NY 10021. Tel. (212) 988-6811.

Page 35 (Neat Feat Treat): Carousel "Yuppy Puppy Doggy Treet" Machine, Carousel Industries, 1757 Winthrop Drive, Des Plaines, IL 60018. Tel. (312) 390-9030 or 1-800-I LUV GUM. **(Buttons and Bones):** Tender Buttons, 143 East 62nd Street, New York, NY 10021. Tel. (212) 758-7004. **(Disney Goes to the Dogs):** *The Disney Book of Knitting*, St. Martin's Press, 175 Fifth Avenue, New York, N.Y. 10010. Tel. (212) 674-5151. Dogwear, 611 Broadway, Suite 702, New York, NY 10012 Tel. (212) 533-0717.

Page 36 (And a Happy New Year): Meowy Chrismouse, Drummer Dancer Dreamer Productions, 87 Columbia Heights, Suite 22, Brooklyn, NY 11201. Tel. (718) 625-0717. **(Beware of Cat...and Dog):** Howard Kaplan's French Country Store, 35 East 10th Street, New York, NY 10003. Tel. (212) 529-1200.

Page 38 (Golden Girl's Generosity): Morris Animal Foundation, 45 Inverness Drive East, Englewood, CO. 80112-5480. Tel. (303) 790-2345. **(Hold That Leopard):** Paul Smith, 41-42-43-44 Floral Street, Covent Garden, London WC2E 9DJ, England, 01-379-7133. Paul Smith, 108 Fifth Avenue, New York, NY 10011. Tel. (212) 627-9770. Paul Smith, 6-3-11 Minami-Aoyama, Minato-Ku, Tokyo, Japan, 4864687. **(Night-table Eating):** Doggie Brown's Gourmet Bones, JW Products Co., P.O. Box 3043, Costa Mesa, CA 92628. Tel. (714) 546-8009. Haute Feline Gourmet Snacks for Cats, L. Coffey, Ltd., 4244 Linden Hills Boulevard, Minneapolis, MN 55410. Tel. (612)

925-3209. Jackie's Cat Snacks, Wagging Tail Ltd., 206 Garden Street, Hoboken, NJ 07030. Tel. (201) 792-5321.

Pages 46-47 (The Two-Party System): Bone Jour Café, 2818 Pennsylvania Avenue, Washington, DC 20007. Tel. (202) 333-8349.

Pages 62-65 (Taking a Cavalier Attitude): The Cavalier King Charles Spaniel Club—U.S.A., Puppy Referral Service, Steve and Anne Shapiro, 12717 Bloomfield Street, Studio City, CA 91604. Tel. (818) 505-1135.

Pages 66-67 (Dress for Excess): Butler and Wilson, 189 Fulham Road, London SW3, England, 01-352-3045. Available at Bloomingdale's and other fine stores. Monty Don, 41 Beauchamp Place, London SW3, England, 01-581-5866. Available at Bergdorf Goodman and other fine stores. Wendy Gell, 37 West 37th Street, New York, NY 10018, Tel. (212) 719-4932. Available at better stores. Kenneth J. Lane, 20 West 37th Street, New York, NY 10018. Tel. (212) 868-1780. Available at better stores.

Pages 68-71 (Take a Walk on the Wild Side): Jim Buck's School for Dogs, 120 East 86th Street, New York, NY 10128. Tel. (212) 860-8680.

Pages 72-73 (Sweater Girls and Boys): Dogwear, 611 Broadway, Suite 702, New York, NY 10012. Tel. (212) 533-0717.

Pages 74-75 (Doggie's Cookies): Lick Your Chops, 1588 1st Avenue, New York, NY 10028. Tel. (212) 988-3900. Lick Your Chops National Sales Office, 299 Main Street, Westport, CT 06880. Tel. (203) 222-8272.

Pages 76-82 (Pawtrait of the Artist as a Young Dog): Paintings by Terry Johnson available at Site, 35 North Main Street, New Hope, PA 18938. Tel. (215) 862-2660.

Page 85 (A Cat for Our Times): Morris the 9 Lives Cat, the Official Spokescat of 9 Lives Food, a division of Star-kist Foods, Inc.

Pages 88-89 (Pretentious Pets): Pretentious Pets, 16 Archery Close, London W2, England, 01-937-2575.

Pages 90-91 (Party Animals): Simplicity Pattern number 8936, available wherever patterns are sold. Simplicity Pattern Company, 200 Madison Avenue, New York, NY 10016.

Page 94 (Wine): Catnip Liqueur available from Cat House Fashions, 307 Hutchinson Road, Englewood, NJ 07631. Tel. (201) 568-1375.

THE NEW